Wilhelm Grütter
in collaboration with
Prof. D.J. van Zyl

THE STORY OF SOUTH AFRICA

Human & Rousseau
Cape Town   Pretoria   Johannesburg

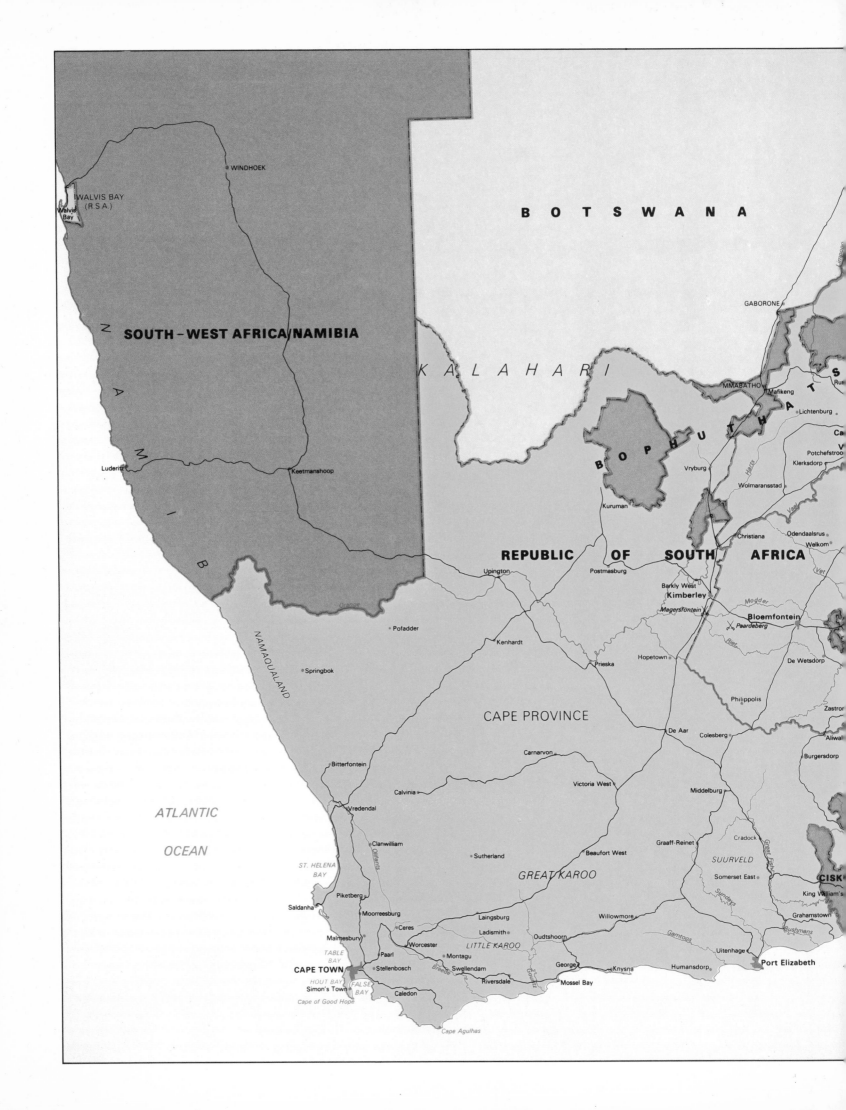

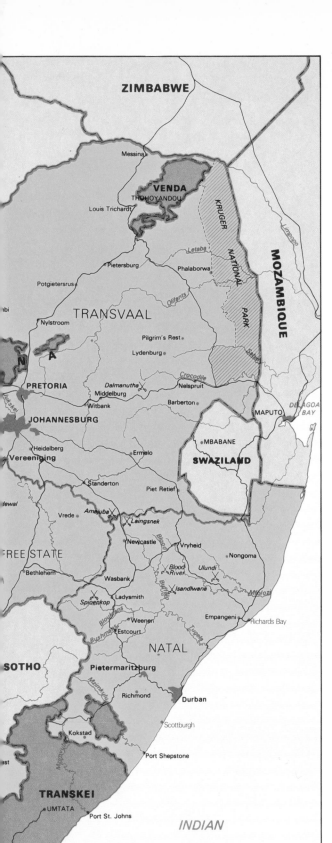

Contents

ISBN 0 7981 1184

First published in 1981 by
Human & Rousseau Publishers (Pty) Ltd
3-9 Rose Street, Cape Town
239 Pretorius Street, Pretoria
112 Pritchard Street, Johannesburg
All rights strictly reserved
Copyright © 1981 by Human & Rousseau Publishers (Pty) Ltd
in conjunction with Gruppo Editoriale Fabbri, Milan
Printed by Gruppo Editoriale Fabbri, Milan

Frail caravels round a continent

The Mediterranean coastline of the continent of Africa as well as part of the east coast had been known and systematically explored since the dawn of civilization and the attendant beginnings of trade. Ptolemy's map of the 2nd century A.D. goes beyond the Horn of Africa in the east, and Greek merchants of the early Roman Empire regularly sailed as far as India, possibly as far south as the Comoro Islands. They certainly made the existence of Zanzibar known to the famous Alexandrian cartographer, but in the west his map barely clears the Canary Islands.

Two pre-Christian voyages of discovery might have extended the bounds of knowledge, but the first has always been regarded as a tall tale, while the second came to naught. Herodotus says that about 600 B.C. Pharaoh Necho sent "Phoenicians with ships, bidding them sail and come back through the Pillars of Hercules (the Straits of Gibraltar) to the Northern Sea (the Mediterranean), and so to Egypt. The Phoenicians therefore set forth from the Erythrean Sea (the Red Sea) and sailed through the Southern Sea (the Indian Ocean). In the third year they turned through the Pillars of Hercules and arrived again in Egypt. And they reported a thing which I cannot believe, but

another man may, namely, that, in sailing round Libya, they had the sun on their right hand."

Most historians today, with Herodotus, doubt this westward circumnavigation of the southern tip of Africa, and latter-day sailors point out that the Phoenician ships were not seaworthy enough to negotiate the Straits of Gibraltar against the prevailing north-easterly winds. Yet there is a strong ring of truth about the Phoenicians' observation that the sun was on their right, as it would have been on their reported voyage up the African west coast. There would have been no reason for them to invent such a monstrous lie.

There is, however, no doubt about the voyage of Hanno the Carthaginian, who, 80 years later, set off down the west coast of Africa with a large squadron to found Punic trading-posts. According to fairly convincing evidence, he made an astonishing advance – as far as the innermost corner of the Gulf of Guinea in the Bight of Benin. But no trading-posts were established, and the silence of centuries fell over the exploration of Africa by this route. Up to the 15th century only a few Italian and Catalonian mariners had ventured occasionally along the west coast into the "Sea of Darkness", never to return.

Rounding Cape Bojador

A single desolate feature on this coast had established itself in the medieval mind as the dreaded point of no return. It was Cape Bojador on the coast of the territory now known as the Western Sahara, about 240 km due south of the Canary Islands. Here, it was believed, a man would be burnt to a crisp by the heat of the sun; the sea would boil away, and monsters would wallow in the ooze. A mysterious magnetic force on the coast would draw any metal out of the ships to split and sink them. And no sailor would dream of circumnavigating Bojador by standing out to sea, for then he would surely fall off the edge of the earth.

It required an exceptional man so to motivate a nation's seafarers as to cause them to shed their fears. He was the Infante Dom Henrique (1394-1460), third son of the Portuguese king João I, later called Henry the Navigator by English historians, although he never made a voyage. Henry, dominated by a fanatical determination to assist Christendom in its religious struggles, dreamt of an alliance with the apocryphal Christian monarch, Prester John of Ethiopia, and had a consuming interest in geography. He was an austere, dedicated man who distinguished himself when the Portuguese took Ceuta from Morocco in 1415. Henry devoted his considerable scholarship to the service of God, hoping to strike down the Moslem infidels who controlled the overland trade routes to the Middle and Far East. He would do this, his priorities ran, "for the glory of God and the profit of Portugal".

Prince Henry established an elaborate fund of seafaring knowledge at his home at Sagres, where all the latest information was studied by teams of cartographers, astronomers and geographers. He had at his disposal various seafaring stalwarts, and regularly sent them forth, armed with the latest intelligence. Under his guidance, Madeira was colonized about 1420, and the Azores in 1427.

"Although he sent out not only ordinary men," wrote Gomes Eannes de Azurara, the prince's personal chronicler, "but such as were of foremost name in the profession of arms, yet there was not one who dared to pass Cape Bojador." In 1433

The voyage of Bartolomeu Dias.

THE WORLD AT LARGE

1498 Christopher Columbus, on his third voyage, discovers Trinidad on 31 July and South America on 1 August.

1524 Giovanni de Verrazano discovers New York Bay and the Hudson River.

1562 Frederick III, the first Calvinist elector in Germany, orders the drafting of the Heidelberg Catechism.

1580 Francis Drake is knighted on completing his circumnavigation of the world, begun in 1577.

1619 Americans hold their first representative colonial assembly on 30 July at Jamestown, Virginia.

Dias was destined to founder in a gale off the cape which he himself had christened "Cabo de Boa Esperança."

Henry dispatched one of his most experienced captains for this purpose: Gil Eannes. But Eannes turned tail at the Canaries. The following year Henry urged him to "strain every nerve to pass that cape. You cannot find a peril so great that the hope of reward will not be greater." In his mind Eannes must have stifled the thought of another peril: that of returning unsuccessfully once again to his stern prince. He shaped a course well out to sea and, when he found a favourable slant of wind, headed eastward for the coast. He found himself about 150 km south of Cape Bojador, and even brought home some plants for Henry. The spell had finally been broken in 1434.

Exploration proceeded apace. In 1441 Antonio Gonçalvez and Nuno Tristão passed Cape Blanco, another 500 km south of Eannes's landing, and brought back gold-dust and slaves. In 1448 Dinis

Dias rounded Cape Verde and penetrated as far as had Hanno the Carthaginian. By the time Prince Henry died in 1460, the Gold Coast and the Slave Coast were firmly in Portuguese hands, were ruled under the patronage of two successive popes, and Henry had been granted the monopoly of the African trade and one-fifth of its profits. For a while business took a back seat to exploration and discovery, while the then ruling monarch, Alphonso V, waged an ideological war against the King of Fez in Morocco.

Exploration continued desultorily, but by 1471 the Portuguese had crossed the equator. Ten years later Alphonso died and his son was crowned João II. He was 26, had long taken a lively interest in his great-uncle Henry's work, and had been in charge of the African trade since his teens. One of his first actions was to confirm Portugal's domination of

the Gold Coast, where, in 1485, he had São Jorge de Mina fortified, this stronghold also serving as a base for further vigorous exploration.

Crosses on southern shores

It was also his idea that his captains should visibly mark Portugal's claim to its discoveries. Tall, two-metre-high columns of limestone (on which appeared his coat of arms, his name, and on which would be carved the name of the explorer and the dates of his voyage) accompanied the expeditions. The columns were surmounted by a cross and were erected on prominent headlands. These famous Portuguese *padrãos* became the first permanent signs of European civilization on the southern shores of Africa.

João's most successful explorer, initially, was Diego Cão, a man of humble birth but exceptional ability, a mercenary without rank or title who was made a knight of the royal household after his first voyage in 1482. In the course of this, in April 1483, he erected a *padrão* at the mouth of the Rio Poderoso, later known as the Congo, and locally as the Zaire. Cão did not return from his second voyage. He probably died near Cape Cross on the barren coast of the Kaokoveld in what is now South-West Africa/Namibia, where he left his fourth and last *padrão* in January 1486.

João might have sensed that success was within his grasp, although he could not have known that Cape Cross was only about 1 500 km north of the cape which was to become the gateway to the east. There are indications that the circumnavigation of Africa had for the first time become an immediate objective in the mind of the king. João certainly lost no time. By 10 October 1486 he had assigned the first ship to an expedition which was to be mounted the following year.

On his return voyage to Portugal, Dias erects his third *padrão* at Luderitz on the coast of South-West Africa. Painting by Charles Davidson Bell, 19th-century Cape artist. (S.A. Public Library, Cape Town.)

That ship was the caravel *São Cristovão*, which was to be prepared by Bartolomeu Dias de Novaes, then an overseer at the royal Guinea warehouses in Lisbon. Little is known of him. He may have been related to Dinis Dias, and it is thought that another relative, João Dias, accompanied Eannes around Cape Bojador. It seems that Bartolomeu was previously involved in the gold and ivory trade on the west coast. Someone of his name was exempted from paying dues on ivory brought back from Guinea in 1478, and he may have been involved in the establishment of Mina in 1481.

Into the gales

In August 1487 Dias left the Tagus with two caravels and a smaller supply-ship. He restocked at Mina, and passed Cão's most southerly *padrão* on 1 December. On Christmas Day, 1487 – the supply-ship having been left behind – Dias reached what later became known as Angra Pequena and is now Luderitz.

He called the bay Angra das Voltas (Bay of Tacks) in exasperation at the endless zig-zagging against head-winds. He continued southward, hugging the coast until, at the end of the first week in January 1488, he probably saw, far inland, what is now known as the Cedarberg mountain range. Dias was then within 320 km of his goal!

But characteristically prevailing southerly head-winds had thoroughly disgruntled him. He decided to seek more favourable winds out to sea, and for 13 days plunged into an ever-strengthening gale in a south-southwesterly direction. Having covered about 1 000 nautical miles, the ships must have been skirting the Roaring Forties before Dias decided to head east again. Had the African coast continued to slant south, Dias would have known fairly accurately where he would meet it again. But when that point arrived, there was nothing. Then he turned north. He had executed a calculated navigational manoeuvre, and had not been blown off course as the historian João de Barros was later to suggest.

The bay of the herdsmen

On 3 February Dias and his men sighted land near modern Mossel Bay, "which we called Angra dos Vaqueiros because of the many cows seen there, watched by their herdsmen", writes Barros. What they saw was probably today's Gouritz River, just west of modern Mossel Bay, which was thus named Rio dos Vaqueiros. The well where they obtained fresh water was known to the Portuguese for over a century as Aguada de São Bras, which commemorated the festival of St Blaise, whose name still exists locally in that of Cape St Blaise, prominent at Mossel Bay.

This was also the scene of the first contact between Europeans and the local inhabitants. Dias bartered for sheep and cattle, but there was an incident which unfortunately ended in violence. Then the ships continued east to Algoa Bay, where Dias christened a small off-shore island "Ilheu da Cruz" (today "St Croix") and was obliged to call a council of officers who decided that they should turn back. Dias persuaded them to follow the coast for a few more days, but was forced to give up at the mouth of the Great Fish River, much to his disappointment.

His two tiny ships were now more than 2 000 km from Cão's last *padrão*, and on 12 March Dias erected one at Kwaaihoek, west of the Bushman's River mouth. This, the earliest known European relic in Southern Africa, was found and restored in 1938, and is displayed in the William Cullen Library of the University of the Witwatersrand.

On 6 June a second *padrão* was set up in the vicinity of Cape Point at the Cape of Good Hope, called by Dias himself "Cabo de Boa Esperança". (Barros ingratiatingly suggested that it was João who was responsible for the name.)

Dias erected his third marker at Luderitz in July, and made his rendezvous with the supply-ship. Only three of her nine men had survived some local hostilities, and Dias took from the ship all the remaining provisions and trade goods before she was burned.

Sixteen months after his departure, Dias came home to the Tagus in December 1488. Despite the tremendous impact his knowledge undoubtedly had, his return was unobtrusive and he received neither recognition nor reward. There is little doubt that, today, his discoveries would have been regarded as intelligence of the highest order. Small wonder, then, that popular maps produced long after Dias's voyage were still based on the incorrect Ptolemaic model. (In 1502 an Italian secret agent, Alberto Cantino, managed to obtain a clandestine copy of the official Portuguese *padron* for 12 gold ducats. This map recorded every one of the new discoveries, and Africa was presented with remarkable accuracy.)

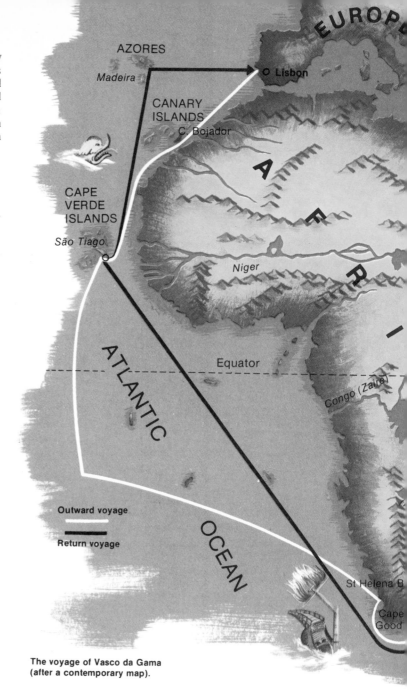

The voyage of Vasco da Gama
(after a contemporary map).

Vasco da Gama

In any event, Portugal's trade on the African coast was highly lucrative, and there was no great hurry to exploit the work of Dias. João II was locked in political struggles with Spain and the pope over spheres of interest. Only after the Treaty of Tordesilhas in 1494 had settled the matter, and Manuel I had succeeded João in 1495, did the route to the east again become a national objective. Manuel continued in the tradition of Prince Henry and for the work of discovery he chose a man who had been born in the year Henry died: Vasco da Gama, a stern disciplinarian, but fair; at times arrogant, but resolute.

Da Gama left the Tagus on 8 July 1497, his flagship being the *nau São Gabriel*. It was accompanied by the *São Rafael* (also a *nau* and armed, like the flagship); the caravel *Berrio*; and a store-ship. Bartolomeu Dias accompanied Da Gama as far as the Cape Verde Islands, where he was to go to Mina to take charge. Da Gama's first landfall in southern Africa was St Helena Bay on the west coast. He arrived on 7 November 1497, 93 days after leaving the islands. He rounded the Cape soon afterwards, on 22 November, and continued along the south-east coast, naming it "Terra do Natal" on Christmas Day. In the middle of February the ships anchored briefly in the mouth of the Zambezi River, reached Mombasa and Arab traders on 14 April, and in Malindi found a pilot to take them across the Indian Ocean. Da Gama anchored in Calicut on the Malabar coast on 20 May 1498. For the Portuguese, the East was won. For Da Gama, a title and the rank of admiral were in sight.

From then onwards the Portuguese made regular voyages, using Mossel Bay and Mombasa as their main staging-posts. But in 1503 Antonio de Saldanha, through a navigational error, sailed into what is now Table Bay. The Cape of

6

Da Gama reaches India, where he hands over credentials from Manuel I, as well as a request that the Portuguese be allowed to trade freely.

Good Hope proper had been discovered, but the bay continued to be known as "Saldanha" for more than a century. It could have been a far more convenient haven for the Portuguese, for the voyage was one of extreme hardship. It is estimated that one ship in ten sailing from Lisbon was lost, and that 60 per cent of the crew died on every voyage. Yet the Portuguese never seriously considered settling at the first safe harbour in the south, the natural halfway point on the profitable spice route.

Yet there were early touches of civilization. In 1500 a fleet under Pedro Alvares Cabral, with Dias commanding one of the vessels, was scattered in a fierce storm off the Cape, having clawed its way back from the coast of modern Brazil. Sadly, one of the ships that foundered was that of Dias. The fleet continued to India, but, on the homeward leg in 1501, touched at Mossel Bay, where one Pedro d'Ataide can be said to have established the first postal service. He left a letter detailing their disasters and this was found by João da Nova on 7 July. Tradition has it that the letter was in a boot hung on a tree, a milkwood tree still standing at Mossel Bay.

English, Dutch and French seafarers

Meanwhile, Portugal's supremacy at sea was crumbling. By 1580 Drake had circumnavigated the globe, and the English, the Dutch, and some French began in increasing numbers to make the spice voyage themselves. Ships meeting one another started the practice of exchanging letters for outward or homeward transmission, while leaving crudely engraved stones on the shores of Table Bay as indications of their passing. The earliest such inscription dates from 1527, and records the fact that David Digaed of Dieppe landed on 10 February. Voyagers also began leaving their letters under such stones, and one of the earliest extant (now in the South African Cultural History Museum in Cape Town), reads: RO(ber)T ADAMS COM(man)D(e)R OF THE BUL(l) AR(r)IVED 29 OF NOVEM(be)R & DEP(art)ED THE 12 OF DE(cembe)R 1619 FOR BANTAM IOS(eph) COCKRAM CAPE MARCH (misspelling of "MERCH(ant)") LETTERS UNDER.

Contact with the local nomadic population was confined to barter and trade on the limited scale required for ships' provisions – there was nothing else on these shores which, to the industrious merchants, was as attractive as the riches they were gaining from the East. There was, therefore, no real incentive to establish a permanent European settlement at the Cape. In addition, the indigenous people were regarded as extremely hostile. And, as now, the southern seas off Africa were gale-swept, and the coast dangerous, as some luckless castaways could testify.

By 1600 the Portuguese were being forced off the scene by the English and the Dutch, particularly (as far as the Dutch were concerned) through the efforts of Jan Huyghens van Linschoten, formerly in Portuguese employ, who gave his countrymen all the Portuguese sailing instructions. As early as 1613 the English briefly considered founding a colony at the foot of Table Mountain, and by 1619 a joint venture was under discussion between the Dutch and English trading companies. However, nothing came of it until much later, when the *Nieuw Haerlem*, a Dutch ship on its homeward journey from the East in 1647, ran aground in Table Bay. The first permanent settlement by Europeans at the southern tip of Africa resulted from a basic error in seamanship!

Bushmen use natural vegetation as a hide in their perennial pursuit of game.

Hunters and herdsmen of the south

The stranding of the *Nieuw Haerlem* on 25 March 1647 brought about the first period of prolonged contact between the voyagers from Europe and the indigenous inhabitants of the southern shores of Africa. It should be remembered that no such scientific discipline as comparative anthropology existed at the time, and naturally Europeans judged the strange people they met by their own social behaviour. The local people, in turn, judged that of the strangers by theirs!

Added to this was the difficulty of communication, since there was no common language. Only one of the local people whom the Europeans met, a man variously called Hadah or Herry, had a smattering of English, apparently acquired when he made a voyage to Bantam in the East, either with John Pynne in 1629, or possibly two years later with John Hall.

This cultural gap, totally unacknowledged well into the 20th century, inevitably became the basis for, at best, misunderstandings, and frequently, at worst, hostilities. It was a pattern which repeated itself all over the world, wherever the supposedly superior, civilized European had dealings with newly discovered peoples.

After the stranding of the *Nieuw Haarlem* about 60 people under command of a junior merchant,

Leendert Janszen, were left at Table Bay to salvage what they could and to fend for themselves, while the remaining two ships, *Oliphant* and *Schiedam*, continued their homeward journey to Holland. Janszen and his men were at the Cape for twelve months, and his diary shows that, while he was cautious in his dealings with the herdsmen from whom he and his men obtained cattle for food, he experienced no untoward difficulties. The herdsmen were kept at a distance from the makeshift settlement, but were always suitably rewarded for whatever they offered. It is significant that not one of Janszen's people was killed by the local inhabitants. On 2 September, however, the aborigines killed a crew member of the *Noordmunster*, which had arrived on 24 August.

Janszen was subsequently asked to report to the Dutch East India Company's ruling Council of Seventeen on the suitability of the Cape as a permanent base. A large part of this report, written by him and Matthys Proot, was devoted to discussing local relationships. Its comments include: "Others will say that the natives are brutish and cannibals, from whom nothing good is to be expected, and that we shall have to be on our guard continually; but this is only a scare story. It is indeed true that also some sailors and soldiers have

been killed by them, but the reason for this is always left unspoken by our folk. Without any doubt, the killing of our folk is rather in revenge for the taking of their cattle, than for eating them. If the proposed fort is provided with a good commander, who treats the natives with kindness, and gratefully pays for everything bartered from them, then nothing whatever would need to be feared."

This view is in sharp contrast to that of most earlier reports. Duarte Pacheco Pereira, initially one of Diego Cão's captains, writes of Mossel Bay: "Whoever goes to this place must beware of the Negroes of this land because they are very bad people, and several times they have tried to kill the crews of ships that go there." On 1 March 1510 the Portuguese viceroy Francisco d'Almeida and about 65 of his men were killed at Table Bay, most probably because of a minor quarrel which led to a retributory attack in which cattle were taken. In 1627 the English seafarer Thomas Herbert was at the Cape and reported: "During the time I staid (sic) amongst them I saw no signs of any knowledge of God, the law of Nature being scarce observed. No spark of Devotion, no symptoms of Heaven or Hell, no place set apart for Worship, no Sabbath for rest."

The Hottentots

None of the earlier reports distinguish between the people encountered. For the most part they are herdsmen, members of various tribes known as Hottentots who, together with the Bushmen, are anthropologically classed today as the Khoisan people. The derivation of the name is clearly described by Augustin de Beaulieu, reporting on voyages in 1620 and 1622: "Their usual greeting on meeting us is to dance a song, of which the beginning, the middle and the end is *hautitou*." Jón Ólafsson (1623) confirms this with: "Their dance was after this fashion. On uttering the word 'Hottentot!', they snapped two of their fingers."

There is no conclusive opinion about the origin of the Hottentots. Current research inclines to the view that they were a racial mixture of Bushmen and Hamites originating in the middle of East Africa in the region of the Great Lakes. From there they migrated southwestward to the west coast of Africa, and thence south to the Cape. Some of them probably moved back to what is today South-West Africa/Namibia, and there are none at the Cape today, as they have been absorbed by other population groups. At the beginning of the 17th century, the Hottentots inhabited the whole of the coastal area from South-West Africa/Namibia eastward to about 28° E.

Traditionally they were nomadic herdsmen and hunters, each tribe living in its own area, one usually circumscribed by its watering-holes and springs. Here, every member of the tribe could live where he pleased, sharing grazing, water and game as common possessions. Just as each clan, consisting of various family units, had a leader, the tribe as a whole submitted to the authority of a chieftain chosen from the most distinguished clan.

Rock paintings from the Clanwilliam district of the Cape Province, possibly made by Bushmen. Such paintings are found in shelters throughout southern Africa. Depicted here are two figures in skin cloaks, with quivers of arrows on their backs. (Tracing by Ione and Hjalmar Rudner.)

Collecting water in ostrich eggs and lighting a fire by friction are the traditional tasks of Bushman women.

A typical Hottentot encampment as seen by Samuel Daniell, the English traveller and artist, in 1801.

Not only do Hottentot burial customs indicate a belief in a clearly expressed form of religion, but there is a strong mythology in which natural elements (celestial bodies and animals) form a harmonious whole with various supernatural beings.

In addition to the hunting life style, the Hottentots shared with the Bushmen a common linguistic heritage. Once again, research is not yet conclusive, but among the similarities in their languages are the morphological and phonetic systems, and characteristic "click" sounds. The Hottentot language has only four, where the Bushmen have five clicks. The grammatical gender of the Hottentots is absent in the Bushmen dialects.

The Bushmen

Bushmen – their name comes from Dutch *bosjes-man* – seem to have occupied large parts of East Africa and even Ethiopia, but began migrating southward under increasing pressure from Hamitic and Negroid groups. They probably occupied the larger part of southern Africa well over a thousand years ago. Bushmen are shy and peaceful ("the harmless people" the anthropologist Elizabeth Marshall called them), and while they must have resented intrusion into their traditional hunting-grounds, they could not have had much contact with early European visitors as they had nothing to barter. Avoiding rather than seeking confrontation, they fell back from White and Black expansion (where they were not ruthlessly hunted into extinction), and today survive chiefly in the Kalahari Desert and some areas of South-West Africa/Namibia.

Their bushcraft and hunting skills – taught to their children from an early age – are almost legendary. Leading a completely nomadic life, protected by only the most rudimentary shelters and clothing, they do not keep animals other than dogs for hunting. The women and children are chiefly responsible for finding edible tubers and wild fruits and berries, as well as water, while the men concentrate on game. They use snares, traps and pitfalls, as well as hides, but their most potent weapon is a bow, equipped with a string made of sinew, and arrows, of which the shaft is usually a light, straight reed without flights. The tips, previously of bone, now of metal, are dipped in various types of paralysing nerve-poisons derived from plants, insects and snakes.

The Bushmen live together in small bands composed of family units, and their only personal possessions are their portable utensils. Hunting-grounds and water are shared by all, and, while a kill belongs to the man who has made it, he always shares it, keeping only the skin and the sinews.

The Bushman's religion has a cosmology similar to that of Hottentot beliefs and has a distinctly monotheistic character.

The Dutch settle at the Cape

In March 1648 five of the ships of the home-bound Dutch fleet took the remaining crew and cargo of the ill-fated *Nieuw Haerlem* back to Holland. One of the ships was the *Conick van Polen*, on which, by coincidence, the young merchant Jan Anthoniszoon van Riebeeck was returning from the East under something of a cloud; he had been accused of trading for his own pocket.

The statement of 26 July 1649 in which Janszen and Proot reported to the Council of Seventeen on the suitability of a settlement at Table Bay was highly favourable: "The soil in the said valley is very good and fruitful, and in the dry season all the water one could wish for could be led through the gardens with little toil. Everything will grow there as well as anywhere in the world. Daily experience teaches us what can be done at the Cape, both for the sick and fit of the crews of ships bound for the Indies, even with only some sorrel and sometimes two or three cattle, since everything is to be had there in sufficient quantity, abundance of fish, and eland and steenbok are abundant. At some seasons of the year there is a quantity of whales, and hundreds of seals. Behind and on the slopes of the Table Mountain there is wood enough available."

It is not beyond the bounds of conjecture that the authors had been given to understand that a favourable report was expected of them; that, in fact, the Council had already made up its mind about settlement. Certainly by the time the Council had come to its decision and drafted a set of instructions in 1651, Proot declined an offer to become commander of the settlement he had so warmly advocated! But Van Riebeeck, anxious for re-employment, offered his services and was appointed after providing thorough and thoughtful comment on the report.

Jan van Riebeeck was born on 21 April 1619 in the small town of Culemborg on the river Lek, to the east of Rotterdam. His father was a surgeon, and this was to be Jan's training as well. At 16 he had already accompanied his father to Greenland and Brazil, and in 1639 he entered the service of the Dutch East India Company as a clerk, soon rising to junior merchant and merchant until, in 1647, in Japan, he was recalled and made a scapegoat. He had to pay a fine, and, although he never succeeded in clearing his name, he was not stripped of pay and title, which would have been the usual procedure had he really been guilty. Van Riebeeck's journal shows that he was a hard-working, conscientious and strict man, but one patient and accessible to those under his command. In accepting the post at the Cape he had only one aim, and that was to be transferred to the East in the Company's service. Of this he first reminded his masters barely two weeks after setting foot at the Cape! He was, however, to remain for ten years.

A garden at the foot of Table Mountain

On Christmas Eve 1651 Van Riebeeck set sail from Texel with his wife, Maria de la Queillerie, and his son of four months. His flagship was the pinnace *Drommedaris*, and the rest of the fleet consisted of the *Goede Hoope*, described as a yacht, the *Reijger* (a flute), and two larger ships, the *Walvis* and the *Oliphant*. Late in the afternoon of 6 April 1652 the first two ships anchored in Table Bay; the skipper of the *Reijger* decided to stand off, and the *Walvis* and the *Oliphant* had been delayed at the start of the voyage. On the following day the company landed, and the last two ships arrived exactly one month later.

Van Riebeeck's instructions were specific: he was not to colonize the Cape. The Council had decided to establish a staging-post only, a "rendez-vous and garrison", and the commander was to build a fort "to be known as Fort de Goede Hoop" and large enough for eighty men. They were to cultivate the land and plant fruit-trees, and ensure that there were pastures. They were to erect a flag-pole from which to signal ships, and build pilot-boats to guide them safely into the bay. They were enjoined to live on friendly terms with the Hottentots, and to barter for livestock sufficient for the Company's needs. And, of course, they were instructed to keep costs down and to become self-sufficient as quickly as possible.

When the ships had left, Van Riebeeck had with him "only ninety poor, ignorant people" who relied on his guidance in everything. But he was a remarkably energetic man, not above grasping trowel or spade himself. Tents were put up as temporary quarters, and, at once, work began on a square fort with earth walls, covered with sods and surrounded by a moat. The ground was rock-hard after a drought; the winter set in before the fort could be completed, and brought rain, hail and bitter cold. (The Cape is an area of winter rainfall, akin to that of the Mediterranean.)

The first attempts to establish a vegetable garden were washed away, and the wife of the senior surgeon died. Yet the first family moved into the fort on 4 June and two days later the settlement

Early painting by Charles Davidson Bell, representing the landing of Jan van Riebeeck at the Cape and his first meeting with the local inhabitants. (S.A. Public Library, Cape Town.)

Ships of the homeward-bound Dutch fleet come to anchor in Table Bay to replenish stocks of fresh food and to rest crews. The VOC emblem of the Dutch East India Company is superimposed on the Dutch ensign.

celebrated its first birth: a boy, Bernert Willemsz, born to the sick-comforter. On 3 August everyone moved into the fort. By this time, almost 20 people had died, and there were many sick.

The tavern of the seas

Yet, when the first homeward-bound fleet arrived under Admiral Gerard Demmer in March 1653, the redoubtable Van Riebeeck supplied it with cattle, sheep, cabbages, carrots and milk, and the admiral complimented him on his fortifications. Van Riebeeck promptly asked for a detachment of sailors to help complete the work, since he was always desperately short of labour. His own work-force was too small, and the Hottentots could not be convinced of the virtues of manual labour. By 1657, Van Riebeeck was forced to import a number of slaves from Java and Madagascar. Meanwhile, he had industriously succeeded in enlarging his gardens and establishing various imported plants

THE WORLD AT LARGE

1652 Rembrandt van Rijn paints the portrait of Hendrickje Stoffels.
1657 Cromwell is installed as Protector of England for the second time.
1661 John Eliot completes the translation of the Bible into Algonquin, this being the first complete Bible to be printed in the American colonies.

and trees. Even vines were planted, and on 2 February 1659 Van Riebeeck happily entered in his diary: "Today, praised be the Lord, wine pressed for the first time from Cape grapes."

But there were disappointments as well. Self-sufficiency seemed unattainable. Wheat proved to be a fickle crop; rice was quite unsuitable; an attempt to export sealskins was a failure; and no precious metals were to be found. While it was always urging the settlement to become self-supporting, the Council provided little help. For some time Van Riebeeck had been asking his overlords to allow free enterprise at the Cape through the establishment of "free burghers" – men who would be entitled to farm on their own account through land grants made by the Company, the Company buying their produce at fixed prices. In a letter dated 30 October 1655, Van Riebeeck was allowed to release officials from their duties for this purpose. But he proceeded with caution. He realized from the outset that this per-mission meant a change of policy; that his staging-post would become a colony. Experimentally, he had leased ten dairy-cows to the Company's gardener, Hendrik Boom, on 1 October 1655, but it was common knowledge that the business providing the settlement and ships with fresh milk was run by his wife, Annatjie. Thus, it was a woman who pioneered free enterprise in South Africa.

In May the following year, wheat, tobacco and beans were sown in areas suitable for cultivation by free burghers, and only when these ventures proved successful did Van Riebeeck grant the first nine men their freedom and their land. This was in February 1657. One of the men, Steven Jansz van Wageningen, was appointed the first burgher coun-cillor and thus became part of the established civil authority.

One problem, however, remained intractable, and this was relations with the Hottentots. Not only did they reject manual labour, but they were not particularly interested in trade. Van Riebeeck had, with great difficulty, established herds of cattle and sheep. But, on 19 October 1653, the tribe known as Strandlopers, led by English-speaking Herry, murdered Van Riebeeck's herdsman, David Jansz, and made off with most of his livestock. On another occasion a group had brazenly started tearing copper buttons from the clothing of children. Van Riebeeck attempted to work out a policy with Rijckloff van Goens, the Company's visiting commissioner, in 1657. On the one hand, he could try to obtain bartering allies by "gentle per-suasion"; on the other hand, he could exclude un-desirables "by means of our fortifications and guard-houses". The first attempt at territorial separation was about to be made.

When Van Riebeeck left the Cape in the *Mars* on 7 May 1662 to become commander and president at Malacca in the Far East, four small forts had been built, and a hedge of bitter almonds had been planted to protect the crops and cattle of the free burghers. Although Van Riebeeck had increased his knowledge and understanding of the sur-rounding Hottentot tribes, continuous petty thievery once led to a fairly serious skirmish on 19 May 1659. But by and large Van Riebeeck could look back on duty well done. By 1658 the settlement consisted of 189 European people – enough for the time being, Commissioner Johan Cunaeus had decided, and Van Riebeeck himself had begun to farm. He was an enthusiastic and successful agriculturalist who passed on his knowledge and experience to the free burghers. While he received little thanks from his lords and masters, who grumbled about his inability to make the Cape profitable, he had unwittingly become the founder of what was later to be a free and independent state.

As early as 1655 Van Riebeeck had realized that his earth-walled fort would have to be replaced by one of stone. But the Castle, today still in use as a military headquarters, was only begun by his successor, Zacharias Wagenaer, on 2 January 1666. The bell-tower (shown here) was completed by Simon van der Stel (governor from 1679 to 1699).

From the time of Jan van Riebeeck's departure to the first British occupation of the Cape in 1795, the settlement continued to be ruled by officials appointed by the Dutch East India Company. Of these, there were no fewer than 26 in the 143 years of Company rule. There were five commanders (one of whom, Simon van der Stel, subsequently became governor, this, from then on, being the rank of the ruling official), and two acting commanders. Apart from Van der Stel, there were twelve governors, two of whom were confirmed in the post after acting in that capacity (Jean de la Fontaine, twice, and Joachim van Plettenberg), and four more acting governors. At the end of the period two joint commissioners-general were appointed, to be followed by Commissioner-General Abraham Josias Sluysken, who was to surrender authority to the British.

It is obvious that not all these men were equally suited to their task, but there were other inherent problems, the main one being the distance from the mother country and the source of policy decisions. Nominally, the Council of Seventeen in Holland directed affairs at the Cape, as they did elsewhere in the far-flung trading empire of the Dutch East India Company, but, in practice, the Cape fell under the authority of the Council of India in Batavia. This was at least 3 months' sailing eastward, and as much as 18 months could pass by before replies were received from Batavia. Another problem was the conflict between the Company's primary purpose, which was profitable trade, and its secondary obligation, which was to provide civil government for the growing colony. Naturally, policy decisions always resolved issues in the favour of trade, and, frequently, this was not necessarily in the interests of those governed.

Van Riebeeck's successor at the Cape was Zacharias Wagenaer, who is chiefly remembered for beginning the building of the Castle on 2 January 1666. It is South Africa's oldest building,

and it is still what it was when it was built – a military headquarters. The principle on which its construction was based was salient bastions (five), from which any attempt to attack the walls could be repelled by raking fire. The Castle was completed in 1678 during the governorship of Johan Bax, and on 26 April the following year the bastions were named after the five earldoms of the Prince of Orange, William III: Oranje, Nassau, Catzenellenbogen, Buren and Leerdam.

Wagenaer's health was poor, and at his own request he was relieved of his post, to be succeeded by Cornelis van Quaelberg in September 1666. During his brief sojourn, Wagenaer had also replaced an unsatisfactory earth dam providing fresh water with a reservoir of stone and brick, and a canal. Remnants of this dam – the oldest remaining Dutch structure in South Africa – were discovered in 1975 during building operations and are today preserved in the Golden Acre, a shopping concourse in the centre of Cape Town.

The Van der Stels

Jacob Borghorst succeeded Van Quaelberg, and was succeeded in turn by Pieter Hackius, Isbrand Goske and Johan Bax. None of their contributions could compete with that of Simon van der Stel, who assumed office on 12 October 1679 and became virtually the second founder of the Cape. He was born in 1639 on the island of Mauritius, where his father was commander. His maternal grandmother, known as Monica da Costa, was of Eastern origin.

Swarthy, cheerful, of medium build, Simon van der Stel was 40 when he arrived at the Cape, and extremely energetic. After quickly attending to his most urgent work, he visited the interior on a five-day journey, begun on 3 November 1679, and decided to establish a settlement on the banks of the Eerste River, calling it "Stellenbosch". Here, where there was less wind, willing free burghers could, he thought, successfully relieve the chronic shortage of wheat. They did. By 1682 Stellenbosch was harvesting one-third of the wheat crop of the Cape. By 1687 the thriving new settlement had a church, a council house, and a residence for the *landdrost* (magistrate), the first local authority outside the Cape.

Van der Stel started a sawmill at Hout Bay, but also encouraged all free burghers to plant oaks. He visited Robben Island to organize fishing and attend to the treatment of convicts, began a brickyard, improved the Castle, and turned his attention to wine. He found the quality "repugnantly harsh" at first, but subsequent vintages, improved by his knowledge, were grudgingly described by Batavia as having a "reasonably good taste". Yet exported Cape wines were far from finding acceptance anywhere, and brandy fared no better. Van der Stel knew how to smelt ore, and had hopes of finding sufficient quantities of copper and silver. He undertook an extensive journey of exploration in the

A Malay school at the Cape in the 18th century. Eventually the Cape Malays became fully indigenous, but preserved their beliefs and traditions. They have contributed a colourful component to the common heritage of South Africans.

THE DUTCH EAST INDIA COMPANY

The Dutch East India Company was established on 20 March 1602, when various small competing trading companies in Holland decided to unite as the *Verenigde Oost-Indische Compagnie* or VOC – known popularly as *Jan Compagnie* or "John Company".

Six of the founding companies formed the constituent chambers of the organization: those of Amsterdam, Zeeland, Delft, Rotterdam, Hoorn and Enkhuizen, and their chief executives became directors of the VOC. Amsterdam nominated 20, Zeeland 12, and the other four chambers 7 each, making a total of 60, of whom 17 became members of an executive committee, the Council of Seventeen. Amsterdam, having provided half the capital, was represented by eight members, Zeeland by four, and the smaller chambers by one each. The seventeenth member was nominated in turn by Zeeland and the small chambers.

The VOC derived its wide authority, which included the right to found and manage colonies, from a charter granted by the States General of the Netherlands at its founding. The Company was given exclusive trading rights east of the Cape for 21 years, this being renewable; it could make trade treaties, and could even declare and wage war in the interests of its trade.

A permanent executive to manage its Eastern interests was instituted by the Council of Seventeen in 1609. From 1619 onwards, when the Dutch drove the British from Djakarta on the island of Java, this Council of India made its permanent home there. It was also known as the Council of Batavia, "Batavia" being the name the Dutch gave to their Eastern headquarters.

The commander (later the governor) at the Cape of Good Hope was an official of the Company. He was assisted by a Council of Policy consisting of Company-appointed officials.

north-west Cape, and organized several other such expeditions. His experience as a captain of mercenary guards in the war against Louis XIV stood him in good stead when he organized the garrison and the burgher militia. And he was usually successful in provisioning passing fleets from the Cape's resources; only rice had to be imported.

In March 1681 life at the Cape was complicated by the arrival of several political deportees from the East: Islamic religious leaders whom the Batavian authorities had found troublesome, and who were put in Van der Stel's charge despite his protests that the Cape had no facilities for dealing with them. How many were sent to the Cape is not known, but the practice persisted until at least 1749. The presence of these exiles became an important cultural factor in the shaping of South African society, for they strengthened the religious and social fabric of other Eastern peoples already living at the Cape.

The first deportees may have arrived as early as 1652; most of them were probably slaves, but there were certainly a number of free artisans among them. This group was significant not only because of their Islamic religion, but because of a distinct way of life that persists to this day. Known as Cape Malays, they were then, as now, skilled in all aspects of the building trade, tailoring, cooperage and basket-weaving, fishing and saddlery, and were South Africa's first true artisans.

Another distinctly non-European race had also by this time emerged. From the earliest time of settlement onward, and in keeping with the policy in Batavia, marriages between the settlers and emancipated Christian slaves or local women had been allowed. Many Hottentots had also become detribalized and were intermarrying with some of the Eastern slaves. In 1682, when visiting the Cape, Governor-General Rijckloff van Goens instructed Van der Stel to oppose all miscegenation, and, when Commissioner Adriaan van Reede inspected the Cape in 1685, such marriages were expressly prohibited unless the female slaves had had Dutch fathers. Nonetheless, a distinct people emerged and became known as Cape Coloureds. (Van Reede also considerably improved the lot of the slaves by providing them with better clothing and housing, and stipulating that their children should be taught by their own teachers.)

The French Huguenots

By 1685 the Council of Seventeen had decided actively to colonize the Cape, and among the groups it encouraged were the French Huguenots who had fled their country after the abrogation of the Edict of Nantes, and had refused to abjure their Protestant religion. An advance party of about 150 French settlers arrived in April 1688 in the *Oosterland* and were given land in the area of Draken- stein, where Van der Stel had already established

In this representation of Greenmarket Square, Cape Town, by the German artist Johannes Rach (about 1764) there is a well- developed town centre dominated by the building (still extant) which housed the Burgher Guard.

26 Dutch smallholdings in 1686. Dutch policy was to absorb the French as quickly and thoroughly as possible, and, while they were free to retain their language and practise their religion in it – they had their own French-speaking pastor, Pierre Simond – Van der Stel did nothing to encourage the perpetuation of a French enclave.

This resulted in a certain amount of friction

between the Huguenots and the governor, but within a generation only the elderly were still using their mother tongue. Today the Huguenot heritage in South Africa comprises a large number of French surnames among the Afrikaans-speaking population, while something of French culture and manners lingers in the exiles' adopted land. The Huguenots did not, however, as is popularly

This memorial to the Huguenot immigrants was dedicated by their descendants in 1948.

13

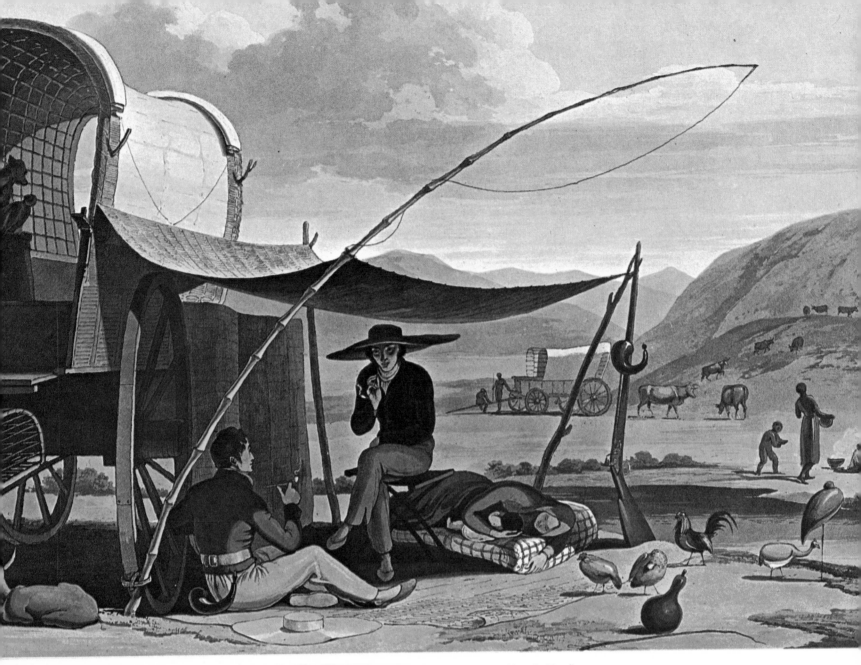

Outspan on Trek **is the title of this painting by the English artist Samuel Daniell, who found that the** *trekboer* **had hardly changed his way of life at the beginning of the 19th century. (S.A. Public Library, Cape Town.)**

believed, contribute much to the quality of South African wine, although, naturally, the quantity rose with the increased amount of land under vines.

Van der Stel had been granted a property of nearly 770 hectares by Van Reede in 1685. This he called "Constantia", and there he enthusiastically began farming. He also built himself a country residence which he often used for entertaining. In 1691 he was promoted to governor, a rank he held until he retired in 1699, being the first important official to adopt the Cape as his new home. When his son, Wilhem Adriaen van der Stel, succeeded his father, the Cape already had a rising birthrate, and population growth was no longer largely dependent on immigration. There were 402 men, 224 women and 521 children.

There were no initial indications that Wilhem Adriaen's rule was to become notorious. He was as industrious as his father and as enterprising, but he was unduly acquisitive, an understandable trait at a time when John Company's officials were underpaid and began exploiting their trading privileges – a growing practice throughout the empire of the VOC. In addition, its regulatory policies concerning trade virtually invited abuse. The economic heresies of the time – monopoly, market manipulation and selective preference –

were John Company's lifeblood. And where private trade and free enterprise were thought expedient, they were controlled by leases which not only raised revenue, but became a potent form of favouritism.

Discontent among the settlers

Despite a ruling, in 1668, that officials were not to own land – Simon van der Stel's grant was an exception – Wilhem Adriaen persuaded Commis-

sioner Wouter Valckenier to let him have 340 hectares in the Hottentots Holland area, and at least seven more officials and Van der Stel's brother, Frans, were also granted land. It is clear from Castle records that Wilhem Adriaen spent much more time on his farm, Vergelegen, than on administering the settlement, and he also made liberal use of servants on the Company's payroll. He began manipulating the granting of licences, particularly in the profitable meat, wine and wheat trade, favouring friends, and discontent among the free burghers grew steadily. Matters came to a head towards the end of 1705, when a petition drawn up by Adam Tas, a Stellenbosch burgher, and signed by 63 malcontents, outlined the burghers' grievances and was sent to Batavia.

Van der Stel got wind of this and hurriedly tried to defend himself, firstly by getting a "testimonial" signed by "supporters" who were entertained at the Castle, and then by arresting and jailing Tas without a warrant on 28 February 1706. On 8 March he made a grievous mistake: he and the Council of Policy decided that five of the complainants should be deported to Holland. They left with the return fleet. Led by Henning Hüsing, who had fallen out of favour and had lost the meat contract on 19 December 1705, the group (one died on the voyage) submitted a damning memorial to the Company, which then appointed a commission of inquiry. Acting on its findings, the Council of Seventeen recalled Van der Stel and three officials to Amsterdam in a letter dated 30 October 1706. It reached Wilhem Adriaen on 17 April the following year.

The free burghers felt that they had vanquished corrupt officialdom, and the celebratory spirit among them ran high for some time. At Stellenbosch in March 1707, young Hendrik Bibault, somewhat in his cups, heckled the unpopular *landdrost*, Starrenburg, and, when asked to behave himself and leave, Bibault shouted: "I will not go! I am an Afrikaner! Even if the *landdrost* kills me or throws me into jail, I will still not be silent!" This is the first time that the use of the word "Afrikaner" was recorded.

Pioneers of the interior

By 1707 the official population of the Cape had risen to 803 adults and 820 children, as against 626 and 521 eight years earlier. They lived at Table Bay or in the neighbouring areas of Stellenbosch, Paarl, Drakenstein and Franschhoek ("French Corner", where most of the Huguenots had been settled). The furthest community was at Roodezand (later called "Tulbagh"), less than 100 km from the Cape.

However, a constant population drift into the interior accelerated at the beginning of the 18th century. There was an overproduction of wine and wheat which, at the Company's fixed prices, were not very profitable crops, while – encouraged by, among others, Governor W. A. van der Stel – more and more farmers were turning to cattle, which required less capital and labour, and were obtainable by relatively profitable barter. Cattle-farming also required extended grazing, and the Company had instituted a system of loan farms – in effect, licences for grazing rights. But, as the farmers had no permanent tenure, they could not subdivide for the benefit of their children.

Thus there came into being the semi-nomadic cattle rancher or *trekboer*, who was constantly in search of better grazing or hunting or both, or moving between summer and winter pastures, and whose children simply trekked even further when they became independent, as it was easy to have new loan farms registered at very low "recognition fees". The *trekboer* developed a strong spirit of self-reliance within the confines of a Calvinist way of life supported by his Bible, as he moved ever further from civilized amenities and from formal religion and education. He also grew increasingly independent of a civil authority which could not be effectively extended over the far-flung areas through which the *trekboer* roamed.

In the north-west and north-east of the colony the *trekboer* waged an all-out war against the Bushmen, virtually exterminating those who did not flee. It was also during the last quarter of the eighteenth century that these farmers first made contact in the east with the Xhosa, who were slowly migrating southward. Occasional disputes about property, grazing and cattle-rustling were settled in punitive skirmishes fought by commandos, voluntary bodies of farmers' militia called out as the need arose. It was only slowly and reluctantly that the Company extended its authority, lagging behind *trekboer* expansion. Swellendam became a magistracy, and the Gamtoos River was declared the eastern border of the colony only in 1745. But by this time *trekboer* pioneers were already at the Great Fish River, which was recognized as the eastern border in 1780, the magistracy of Graaff-Reinet being established in 1785. By then the

trekboer had identified himself with Africa for several generations and, through his isolation, had developed into a distinct pioneering type. He was to become the core of the individualistic Afrikaner people.

Probably the most popular and successful governor of the Cape during the long and uneasy decline of the VOC after its first 50 years of expansion was Ryk Tulbagh. A Company official at the Cape since 1718, he was sworn in as governor on 27 February 1751. He was a cultured and widely read man who impressed distinguished foreign visitors. His botanical work won him European recognition, and it was he who founded the first lending library at the Cape in 1761.

Tulbagh was a conscientious administrator. His most important task was the codification of the slave laws, which had proliferated since the founding of the Cape and were thoroughly confused. By then there were about 5 000 adult slaves at the Cape (the free population being only about half that size), and they were sometimes very troublesome. Tulbagh's code was strict, in accordance with prevailing thought. Slaves could still, however, obtain their freedom by purchase or as a reward from their owners. Once free, they were treated in every way as the equals of the local inhabitants.

In 1755 there was a serious outbreak of smallpox at the Cape, and it is estimated that nearly 1 000 settlers and well over 1 000 slaves lost their lives. How many Hottentots perished will never be known, but it is certain that this scourge substantially reduced their chances of survival. A second epidemic struck in 1768. This Tulbagh tried to combat as energetically as he did the first.

He had no time in which to attend to 124 regulations which, issued in Batavia, were meant to restrain the extravagances of local officials. They had been forwarded to him by the governor-general, Jacob Mossel, with the request that they should also be applied at the Cape. Tulbagh ordered three of his councillors to prepare an adaptation of these so-called sumptuary laws for local use. Yet he has gone down in South African history as the man who promulgated laws restricting "pomp and splendour".

Tulbagh's governorship was plagued by an

Part of a sketch by the English traveller W. J. Burchell. It depicts a *trekboer* encampment in the north-western Cape.

GABLES DENOTE A DISTINCTIVE ARCHITECTURAL STYLE

The development of the distinctive Cape-Dutch style of architecture can be followed in the so-called "letter layout" of the floor plans, and in the emergence of gracefully proportioned gables which still adorn historic homesteads.

Initially, houses consisted of three simple rooms, end to end, with the long side facing the street. Subsequently, a room or two might be added as a wing at one end, resulting in an L-plan, while another wing on the other side resulted in a U enclosing a courtyard on three sides. Further inland, the "wing" tended to be built from the middle of the house towards the back, the result being a T-plan, and, when further expansion was required, a row of rooms was added at the foot of the T, the home then representing an H-plan.

Ultimately, gables were used above the central front entrance both as a visual embellishment and as a means of admitting light to the loft.

The farmhouse at La Provence, near Franschhoek, provides one of the finest examples of the early neo-classical gable. This development of the Cape-Dutch style came into vogue at the beginning of the 19th century.

economic depression which was relieved chiefly by the outbreak of the Seven Years War between Britain, France and Spain (1756-1763). The Cape soon saw many foreign ships that required victualling, this becoming perhaps the first proof of its strategic importance.

Ryk Tulbagh died on 11 August 1771. He was known affectionately as "Father Tulbagh" by the colonists, and he is commemorated in the name of the town that was founded at Roodezand in 1795.

The last years of Company rule

The last years of the Company's rule at the Cape reflect the acceleration of its decline (the VOC paying its final dividend in 1782). There was an increasing spirit of rebelliousness among subjects who had to fight the first full-scale war against the

Xhosa at the Great Fish River in 1779, and who were influenced by events in Europe.

The VOC had been weakened by official corruption and wars, and was successfully ousted from the India trade by the British. Its citizens at the outposts of the Cape were demanding adequate protection, and throughout the colony revolutionary ideas about democratic government were on the increase. The influence of European thinkers such as Locke, Grotius and Pufendorf was beginning to make itself felt among free burghers who wanted political rights guaranteeing their economic interests. They expressed their views by circulating clandestine writings, and by holding secret meetings.

A group known as the Cape Patriots brought matters to a head when a free burgher at the Cape was banished to Batavia without trial in January 1779. The Patriots sent a delegation to Holland and presented a bulky petition to the Council of Seventeen on 16 October. This detailed not only

common complaints against Company price-fixing and corrupt officialdom, but, in 37 articles, demanded a number of civil liberties. The Council reacted only in December 1783, and, to various other requests, up to two years later. The Patriots did not gain any significant concessions and continued their agitation.

In the border areas the chief cause of dissatisfaction was the Company's inability to protect the farmers, while at the same time it followed a conciliatory policy towards the Xhosa. In 1795, the year in which the British first took over the Cape of Good Hope from the Dutch, open rebellion broke out. On 6 February armed farmers ordered the unpopular *landdrost*, H. C. D. Maynier, to leave his office at Graaff-Reinet, called themselves the "general voice of the people", elected their own representatives, and resisted attempts by an official to persuade them to recognize the Company's authority. On 17 June the burghers of Swellendam followed suit, forcing the *landdrost*, A. A. Faure, to relinquish his post. They established a revolutionary national convention, declaring that they intended to govern themselves. Events were to overtake them, but these first flickerings of republicanism were destined never to die.

Meanwhile, the French Revolution of 1789 had set in motion a train of events that was to change the course of history at the southern tip of Africa, as elsewhere. Europe became engulfed in the revolutionary wars, and Prince William V had to flee from Holland to England in January 1795. In the Netherlands French forces established a Batavian Republic in accordance with the ideals animating the French Revolution.

A strong British fleet was soon sent to occupy the Cape before the French could do so, and the commissioner-general of the VOC at the Cape, Abraham Sluysken, was asked by the Prince of Orange to regard the British as friends. Admiral Elphinstone and General Craig arrived in False Bay on 11 June 1795, but were opposed by Sluysken and about 2 500 men, militia as well as burghers. During a troubled month, some inconclusive and half-hearted fighting took place. Disheartened burgher forces, suspecting treachery among their leaders, who were plagued by loyalties divided between the monarchy, on the one hand, and republican ideals, on the other, finally retreated. On 16 September 1795 Sluysken capitulated. Almost a century and a half of VOC rule at the tip of Africa had come to an end.

The Cape Colony about 1750. The dates at the ends of the arrows on the map indicate when the *trekboer* pioneers reached various areas.

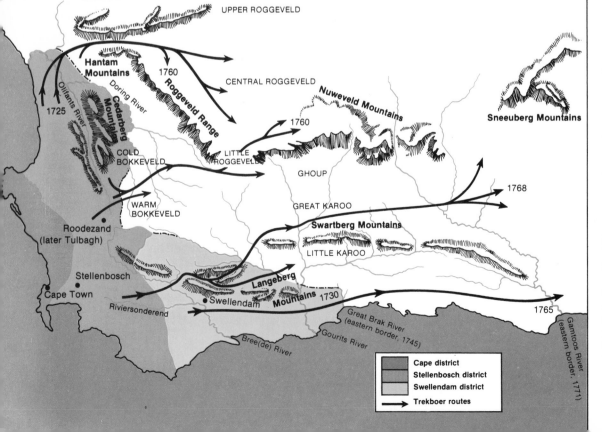

British caretakers and a Dutch interlude

Earl Macartney, the first British civil governor of the Cape.

For the first time since its inception the Cape was now governed by a civil administration controlled by the British Colonial Office. Initially there was a military government under Craig and Elphinstone, and general Clarke, who was sent with a force of 3 000 men to help them take the Cape. With the departure of Clarke and Elphinstone on 15 November 1795, James Henry Craig was in sole charge. The terms of capitulation had been sensible and lenient. Although the colonists were required to take an oath of allegiance to Britain, Cape laws and customs remained unaltered, no new taxes were levied, monopolies were cancelled, internal and external trade restrictions were swept aside, land rents in arrears were remitted, and goods from any part of the British possessions were admitted free of duty (this subsequently being limited to goods from Britain only).

The internal economy of the Cape was still unstable, but there was a distinct economic revival due chiefly to the large military presence and the war in Europe, which stimulated external trade and virtually doubled shipping. During the first British regime 170 ships called annually at the Cape, as against only 86 in 1794, when VOC activities had slackened. The oath of loyalty was not an obstacle to most citizens, apart from those of Graaff-Reinet, where the writ of the British ran only a year later after a show of force by Craig, and where trouble was again to develop. The population of the Cape Colony has been estimated to have been between 16 000 and 20 000 Europeans, 17 000 to 25 000 slaves and about 15 000 Hottentots.

Craig governed firmly and energetically. In May 1797 he was succeeded by Earl Macartney, a 60-year-old conservative who loathed the ideas of the French Revolution and had been a British envoy in Russia and China, as well as a governor of Madras. With his experience in civil government, he provided an administration that was efficient and above reproach, but he relied on a form of coercion thoroughly hateful to the colonists. He used to

billet soldiers on them as a punitive measure – if, for example, they failed to deliver their quotas of wheat to the government – while Hendrik Eksteen, a supporter of the Cape Patriots, once had to endure this punishment for using the word "citizen" on invitations to his daughter's wedding.

Major-General Francis Dundas acted as governor for a year after Macartney had left on 20 November 1798, and he was succeeded by Sir George Yonge on 10 December 1799. Yonge has been described as "a hoary old jobber", and seems to have been thoroughly inept and badly advised.

Yonge, however, faced serious problems. From 1798 onwards there had been three successive crop failures, and in 1800 he averted famine only by importing rice and putting the garrison (4 600 people, including women and children), the fleet (3 000 officers and men), and the townspeople (16 000 souls) on limited allowances of bread made of mixed wheat and barley. He did his best to establish a fishing industry, and tried to introduce modern farming methods by establishing the country's first experimental farm at Klapmuts under a knowledgeable superintendent, William Duckitt, who arrived on 11 September 1800. But these ventures failed, and Yonge was recalled in disgrace, relinquishing his duties on 20 April 1801. He had also made the mistake of introducing new taxes, the colonists being particularly outraged by his game licences and an increase in the duty on brandy. Once again Dundas took over.

Trouble on the frontier

The eastern border remained troubled throughout the first British administration. Macartney's secretary had been John Barrow. He remained as an official, but was unsympathetic to the colonists. He should not, therefore, have been sent to the border in 1797 and, on his return, his hostile attitude to the farmers, and his support for conciliatory overtures to the Xhosa, misled authorities who were trying to ease the situation. Matters came to a head with the arrest of a Graaff-Reinet burgher, Adriaan van Jaarsveld, on a charge of having forged a receipt. His compatriots regarded this as a pretext, broke into open rebellion, and freed him. It was only in March 1799 that General Vandeleur subdued the insurrection.

By then, however, civil unrest had encouraged the Xhosa who were on the European side of the Great Fish River to join the Hottentots in raiding

farms and seizing cattle. Influenced by Barrow and Maynier, whom the British had reinstated as the *landdrost* at Graaff-Reinet, Dundas would not allow Vandeleur to take any military action. Instead, the governor himself went to the border on a peace mission in September 1799. This left the farmers thoroughly dissatisfied as the Xhosa were allowed to continue to occupy the Suurveld, west of the Great Fish River.

Whatever the merits of Dundas's and Maynier's border policy, it was doomed to failure for lack of a proper police force. By October 1801 the burghers of Graaff-Reinet had once again taken up arms. They besieged the magistracy, and demanded Maynier's recall. Dundas acquiesced, after sending a force to restore order, but the chaotic situation on the border continued. Hundreds of homes and farms had been burnt and the frontiersmen were demoralized. By the middle of 1802 Dundas had made another attempt to restore peace, but he succeeded merely in obtaining an agreement that the various groups would stop molesting one another, when full-scale military action would have been the only solution (the Xhosa regarding negotiations as a sign of weakness).

But Dundas was content. He already knew that the Cape was to revert to the Dutch as a result of the Treaty of Amiens (28 March 1802). The problem was no longer his, although, in Britain, the desirability of permanently occupying the Cape had been considered. In a remarkably prescient communication to Dundas on 10 July 1797, Macartney had said that "its (the Cape's) chief importance to us arises from its geographical position, from its forming the master link of connection between the western and eastern world, and, above all, from the conviction that, if in the hands of a powerful enemy, it might enable him to shake to the foundation, perhaps overturn and destroy the whole fabric of our oriental opulence and dominion."

The Dutch return to the Cape

The briefly renewed Dutch administration of the Cape did not succeed in resolving the border problem. Its duration was even shorter than that of the first British occupation. This was unfortunate, because this administration promised to be the kind of civil government which might have developed into a model of enlightened control. It began on 23 December 1802, when the commissioner-

A view of Cape Town from the Castle walls, painted by Lady Anne Barnard, wife of the Colonial Secretary, and official hostess in Macartney's time. In the foreground is the Parade, where military exercises were held. It contained a gallows, and was surrounded by the barracks, the hospital and slave-quarters.

General Janssens meets the Xhosa chieftain Ngqika on the eastern border. The governor is accompanied by an armed guard, Ngqika by a long train of subjects.

general, Jacob Abraham de Mist, and the governor, Lieutenant-General Jan Willem Janssens, arrived, formally to assume responsibility for the Cape in the name of the Batavian Republic on 21 February 1803. De Mist was a member of the Council for the Asiatic Possessions (the equivalent of a Colonial Office). Even before the Treaty of Amiens had been signed, he had prepared such a thorough memorandum on the possible management of the Cape that he had been given the job. He ranked above Janssens, initially a professional soldier who, however, proved to be an efficient civil servant. De Mist's ideals are clear from his memorandum: "All the sins of the past, those of omission and of commission, can now be wiped out as with a damp sponge, and on the clean white page may be written the new Charter for this settlement, framed with wisdom, mildness and discretion, but always tempered with a proper firmness." He had not been to the Cape before, but had based his observations on published works and official documents. Practical experience caused the modification but not the abandonment of ideas which, imbued chiefly with the liberalism of the French Revolution, were to be applied by a firm central government.

De Mist retained the supreme authority of his office, but delegated legislative and executive authority to his governor, Janssens, and a Council of Policy of four members, of whom at least two had to be burghers who had been resident at the Cape for at least 16 years. Each had specific portfolios: agriculture and animal husbandry, finance, trade, and shipping and fisheries. Another important innovation was the establishment of an Accounting Chamber. Its members were appointed by the Asiatic Council, and, although ranking below those of the Council of Policy, were responsible only to the former body. Thus the colony's finances could not be abused by the government, and the colonists enjoyed the application of the principle "no taxation without representation". An equally independent Council of Justice was formed, its right of appeal being to the Supreme Court at The Hague.

Having laid the foundations of a strong and impartial central government, De Mist soon realized that local authority would have to be improved if the extensive colony was to be governed effectively at a day-to-day level. At the Cape he instituted the Community Council, elected by the ratepayers, and thus created the country's first system of municipal government. Both De Mist and Janssens undertook a lengthy journey in the interior to inform themselves at first hand of conditions. They soon saw that the four existing districts (Cape Town, Stellenbosch, Swellendam and Graaff-Reinet) were much too unwieldy for efficient administration, and, in 1804, proclaimed two more – Tulbagh and Uitenhage. A *landdrost* was appointed in each, he being assisted by six local citizens (*heemraden*) and a secretary, their limited powers being carefully circumscribed. Another innovation, and a great relief in the outlying districts, where there were few ministers of religion, was the power of the *landdrost* to solemnize marriages. He was helped to maintain law and order by several field-cornets, government appointees who did not receive a salary, but who were exempt from taxes.

Unsolved problems

In his church ordinance of 1804, De Mist extended equal legal protection to all religious denominations. This, and the new dispensation for marriages, some of the more conservative inhabitants found too liberal. But he had not yet done. In the same year he promulgated an ordinance which removed education from the direct control of the church to that of the state. But this effort to provide a uniform standard had not yet been properly implemented when the Batavian regime came to an end.

Three successive crop failures bedevilled wheat-farming, but De Mist made every effort to improve other types of agriculture. A wine expert from the Rhineland was brought to the Cape, this resulting in some improvement in the quality of the vintages,

but not in profitable exports. The administration tried to introduce farmers to the advantages of improving wool production through Spanish merinos – even importing a few rams at government expense – but, on the whole, found the sheep-farmer too set in his ways.

The thorniest problem remained the relationship between the settlers and the Xhosa on the eastern border. Liberal-minded people like De Mist and Janssens were influenced by the views of Rousseau, embodied in his concept of the "noble savage", but realities began to temper their outlook. The Xhosa were then well established on the west bank of the Great Fish River, and Janssens went to negotiate with their local chief, Ndlambe, who was willing to cross the river and to acknowledge it as the boundary between the Cape Colony and his own people, after his enemy, Ngqika (also known as Gaika), had been vanquished. Negotiations with Ngqika proved fruitless, for, although he was willing to accept the boundary, he was not interested in a peace with Ndlambe. There was little more that could be done, and Captain Ludwig Alberti was stationed in the area with a small force and orders to maintain absolute territorial separation between the colonists and the Xhosa. But the problem was still not solved.

A fair amount of attention was paid to the grievances of the Hottentots, who were given the protection of a contract which had to be signed before a *landdrost* if they were taken into employment by farmers; and, although De Mist was not entirely convinced that the work of some missionary societies among the Hottentots was beneficial, he set aside large tracts of land for this purpose. He also intended abolishing slavery by freeing the children of slaves as they were born, but, once again, the regime was too brief for the intention to become effective.

There is no telling where all these reforms might have led, given more time, and allowing for the fact that many of them were regarded as too liberal to be popular. But the Batavian organizational structures for the districts were later to survive significantly in the country's history, when some of them were adopted by the leaders of the Great Trek.

New masters from Britain

The arrival of the British settlers in Algoa Bay in 1820 strengthened the small frontier community, hastened the process of Anglicization, and added yet another cultural entity to the plural society of South Africa. (After a painting by Thomas Baines.)

The peace between Britain and France did not last for long, and the governor, Janssens, soon had to prepare for a possible attack on the Cape by the British. On 7 January 1806 a fleet of 61 British ships, carrying 6 700 men under Major-General Sir David Baird, anchored in sight of Table Mountain, off Blouberg Strand. The naval commander was Sir Home Popham, inventor of the modern flag-signalling system. Janssens had a force of only 2 000 mixed levies; the outcome of the battle was a foregone conclusion. Janssens capitulated on 18 January, when the customary guarantees preserving the rights, privileges and religion of the colonists were provided, but there were no guarantees about the continuation of laws and customs, or the non-imposition of new taxes.

The initial military government was soon replaced by civil authority, and the second British occupation of the Cape was confirmed in 1814, when the colony was formally ceded to Britain under the Convention of London.

Inevitably, British rule meant the introduction of British views and culture, often with far-reaching effects. The British ruling class was conservative, if not downright reactionary, and firm believers in keeping the common people in their place. This was soon to become one of the root causes in awakening a growing feeling of national identity among the Dutch population which was to lead, a few decades later, to the Great Trek.

British rule was also firmly autocratic, with the governor in charge of the legislative, executive and judicial functions, without even an advisory body to check his absolute authority. Correspondence between the Cape and Europe could take up to six months for a single exchange of letters, and thus local government was fairly arbitrary.

THE WORLD AT LARGE

1807 Robert Fulton's steamboat, the *Clermont*, begins to ply the Hudson River.
1815 18 June: Wellington and Blücher defeat Napoleon at Waterloo.
1829 The first boat-race between Oxford and Cambridge takes place.
1841 The *New York Tribune* is founded.
1852 30 June: A British Act of Parliament institutes representative government for New Zealand.

Alienating the non-British population (by this time the embryonic Afrikaner nation) as much was a firm insistence on Anglicizing all aspects of government, as well as education and religion. A third factor was the rise of the influential philanthropic movement in Britain, which at the Cape often fostered the interests of the non-European races at the expense of the White colonists. This, probably, was the greatest single source of grievance against British colonial policy among the Afrikaners.

When Baird took over in 1806, the Cape was an extensive area sparsely inhabited by about 26 000 Europeans, with a large slave population of about 30 000, and probably about 20 000 Hottentots. The British authorities cared little about the development of the Cape interior, regarding it as worthless and barren. To them, the colony was "the Gibraltar of the Indian Ocean". There was no expenditure on development, and, by 1814, when the artificial stimulation of the economy caused by the European wars had ceased and garrisons had been almost halved (and the Cape had endured its usual dismal run of crop failures), the colony was facing economic collapse. Matters were not improved when the British began issuing paper money.

19

SLAVE EMANCIPATION

Slavery at the Cape was almost as old as the colony itself, and, by and large, successive administrations had provided for humane practices in terms of the times. The philanthropist movement, however, coupled the Cape with the West Indian colonies, where slavery existed in all its inhumanity, and was defended in Britain by powerful sugar interests.

Thus, while there was every evidence that slaves at the Cape were well treated (as the important social and economic asset which they were), a series of slave regulations affecting the colony did not take local conditions into account. By 1807 the philanthropic lobby had succeeded in securing the abolition of the slave trade in the British Empire, and concentrated its efforts on slave treatment. Thus, in 1816 Somerset ordered the registration of slaves to prevent importation by smuggling, and in 1820 Bathurst would not allow the British settlers to use slave labour. A series of slave regulations, tightly circumscribing their treatment, were in force until 1832.

In 1833 the British parliament passed the Emancipation Act, which also abolished slavery at the Cape from December 1834. While there was compensation for slave-owners, the amounts and methods of payment caused dissatisfaction among the Dutch population. Owners were lucky if they received £41 for every £100 of their investment; the 35 745 slaves at the Cape were independently valued at £3 041 249, but only 41 per cent of this sum was made available for compensation payments to be issued in London, and in British government stock at that. Being inexperienced in such matters, and lacking any London representation, most of the Dutch slaveowners were forced to sell their claims to agents at a considerable loss.

Centralized rule

The beginnings of efficiently centralized rule were introduced by the first British civilian governor, the Earl of Caledon, who arrived at the Cape in May 1807. He created three more districts – Clanwilliam, George and Caledon, and in 1811 instituted a circuit court which, annually, visited outlying districts. This court not only dealt with matters outside the jurisdiction of the *landdrost* and *heemraden* established by the Dutch, thus improving the administration of justice, but reported on educational, religious and social conditions in the more distant areas, thus becoming an integral part of the policy of centralization. The circuit court was a useful institution, but because of its zeal in protecting the indigenous people and the slaves, it was regarded with distrust by the Cape Dutch, particularly after the so-called "Black Circuit" of 1812, which heard an inordinate number of cases concerning non-Whites.

In 1806 the position of the Hottentots was that of a landless proletariat. This Caledon tried to remedy by a proclamation which, in 1809, recognized them as British subjects, and which provided for the registration of their labour contracts. In Britain, the influential philanthropic movement, stressing universal equality and the inviolability of human worth, exerted increasing pressure through the Colonial Office to secure the rejection of any practice seemingly in conflict with these ideals. Spurred on by its local representatives, the London Missionary Society succeeded in convincing the British government that grievous injustices to the Hottentots were perpetrated at the Cape, and the Colonial Secretary ordered a thorough investigation. Thus the "Black Circuit" Court of 1812 spent more than four months investigating allegations of crimes and injustices perpetrated by the colonists. More than 50 colonists were brought to court, and more than a thousand witnesses were called. The philanthropists had maintained that in one district alone over 100 murders of Hottentots had gone unpunished, yet only 17 cases were brought before the court, and not one of the charges was upheld. Some fines were imposed for harsh punishment and lesser offences, but the Cape Dutch were outraged. Affronted by the accusations, they had suffered great inconvenience in answering the charges, and regarded the British and all they did with even greater distrust and suspicion.

Finally, as a result of further zealous propaganda, Ordinance 50 was issued in 1828. Rightly known as the Magna Carta of the Hottentots, it granted them non-discriminatory treatment and total freedom of movement. It increased vagrancy and theft and exacerbated labour problems. It was also a turning-point in non-White legislation, which from then was to be "colour-blind" at the Cape.

Unrest on the frontier

Lord Charles Henry Somerset became governor on 6 April 1814. He was a member of an influential aristocratic family, a prototype of the Tory reactionary, and a man of autocratic leanings. He was destined to come into sharp conflict with the Cape Dutch, just as he subsequently did with not only the British settlers who arrived during his term of office, but even with the philanthropists. Early in his governorship there occurred what has been described as "the unsavoury Slagtersnek incident" of 1815. A farmer at Graaff-Reinet, on the eastern frontier, Frederik Bezuidenhout, had ignored a summons to appear before a court on a charge laid by a Hottentot labourer. He was sentenced in his absence, and the *landdrost* sent a small force to arrest him. When he resisted, he was shot and killed. To make matters worse, the force consisted of four White and twelve Hottentot soldiers, and it was one of the latter who fired the fatal shot.

The dead man's brother swore vengeance, and began an insurrection in alliance with some of the less desirable frontier elements, even asking the Xhosa chief, Ngqika, for support. Their force of about 60 surrendered on 18 November 1815, and the six leaders were sentenced to death by the special court appointed by Somerset, who made it clear that he expected vigorous justice to be meted out. The sentence of one of the accused was commuted on the grounds of old age, but on 9 March 1816 the other five were hanged – four of them twice, as the nooses broke at the first attempt. This was an emotional incident certain to inflame tempers, although many frontier farmers did not agree with the rebels' behaviour.

Settlers from Britain

With the end of the Napoleonic Wars in 1814 and the growth of the Industrial Revolution in Britain, there was widespread unemployment and poverty, and many people saw emigration as their only hope. At the Cape, the border conflict between the settlers and the Xhosa was becoming more dangerous with every year. This inspired Somerset to ask the British government to encourage settlement in the eastern frontier districts of the Cape. Conditions for would-be emigrants were fairly favourable, and soon about 4 000 applications out of a

A group of British settlers (possibly a family named Bowker) encamped at the Great Fish River. (A painting by F. T. l'Ons, a settler from Islington.)

Among the numerous clashes between the Whites and the Xhosa was the Seventh Frontier War, or the War of the Axe, which began when a chief, Sandile, refused to hand over a follower who had allegedly stolen an axe at Fort Beaufort. This scene depicts the battle at the Gwanga River on 8 June 1846, when British troops commanded by Colonel Henry Somerset drove back a strong Xhosa force. The war lasted until 1848. (Painting by H. Martens.)

torrent of almost 90 000 were approved by the British government.

The first group of British settlers arrived in Algoa Bay (at what is now Port Elizabeth) on 9 April 1820. There they were personally welcomed by the acting governor, Sir Rufane Donkin. Unfortunately, most of them were tradesmen and city-dwellers. Their lack of farming knowledge and of local conditions, as well as inadequate government guidance and a series of agricultural disasters, made life very difficult for them. Only about 40 per cent of the first settlers persisted as farmers. They became relatively well-off as time passed, and, with Spanish merinos, established a viable wool industry. The other settlers reverted to their original trades or entered commerce, mostly with success.

Naturally, the settlers reinforced the British government's policy of Anglicization, a policy officially sanctioned in July 1822. From 1825 onwards, English was the sole language used by government officials, and, from 1827 onwards, the sole language of the courts as well. The Dutch kept quiet. Most of them never abandoned their mother tongue, but did become bilingual.

Meanwhile, the British settlers quarrelled with Somerset on two issues: his authoritarian handling of judicial and land matters, and his opposition to a free press. By 1823 Britain had sent a commission to the Cape to investigate the settlers' grievances, most of which were upheld. Somerset – who was in England at the time – was compelled to resign in April 1827. His departure was regretted neither by the British settlers nor by the Cape Dutch, whom he had also tried to Anglicize by importing Presbyterian clergy from Scotland and teachers from Britain.

The establishment of the British settlers on the eastern border as a bulwark against the Blacks was largely unsuccessful, and subsequent border policy hovered between firm local action, frustrated by the influence of the British philanthropists, and attempts at total territorial separation. The Colonial Office could hardly be expected to understand conditions on such a distant frontier, and, with the exception of Somerset, few governors remained at the Cape for any significant length of time. They stayed no longer than was necessary to shed preconceived ideas and to adopt more balanced points of view – and then left. Consequently, British frontier policy was characterized by vacillation; interpreted by the Xhosa as weakness, this led to frequent and sometimes serious clashes.

First experience of parliamentary government

In 1834 Sir Benjamin D'Urban, who had assumed the office of governor on 10 January, instituted a legislative council consisting of a number of government officials and colonists appointed by the governor. Although real power was still firmly vested in the governor and his officials, the freedom of citizens to debate public affairs was established, and the local population gained their first experience of a rudimentary form of parliamentary government.

An event which really united the citizens of the Cape – British and Dutch – on an issue of public importance, was the decision by the British government, in 1849, to use the Cape as a settlement for convicts from the British Isles. The local population were furious, and there were wholesale resignations from public bodies.

It soon became clear that the British government intended to persist with the policy of establishing a penal settlement at the Cape. A ship with 282 convicts on board had already arrived in Table Bay. The public outcry forced the government at the Cape to change its policy, and the ship, and its hapless convicts waiting to disembark, set sail for Tasmania early in 1850. This powerful expression of public opinion hastened the constitutional development of the Cape, and in 1853 the first elections for a Cape parliament were held.

PRINGLE AND FAIRBAIRN FIGHT FOR A FREE PRESS

Thomas Pringle and John Fairbairn were two settlers with a talent for the pen rather than the plough. Together with the printer George Greig they published the first real newspaper at the Cape, The South African Commercial Advertiser, a weekly which first appeared in 1824 despite Somerset's opposition. Pringle, in conjunction with Dr Abraham Faure, a minister of the Dutch Reformed Church, also published a quarterly, The South African Journal. They soon incurred Somerset's displeasure. At first the governor attempted to impose a censorship, and then he issued an outright ban. This was withdrawn for a period by the Colonial Secretary, Earl Bathurst, but was imposed again in 1826. At various times Greig, Pringle and Fairbairn joined the agitation in London against the autocratic governor, and in 1828 the government issued an ordinance which became the foundation of a free press, and which was to be subject only to the laws of libel.

Blacks in search of better grazing about 1803 - a contemporary gravure in colour.

The Black people of South Africa

The largest indigenous peoples in Africa today are the Bantu, the Negroes and the Hamites. (The designation *Bantu* is derived from the word for "people" in the Black languages of southern Africa, and it specifically means Black people. The term was coined by the 19th-century philologist Bleek.) The Negroes, traditionally agriculturalists, have been living in the tropical forests of Africa for thousands of years, and the Hamites and their cattle seem to have entered Africa from the east and spread over North Africa. Separated by the Sahara Desert, the two groups first made contact in the region of the Great Lakes, north of the equator. This resulted in the birth of a third ethnic group, the Bantu, who adhered to the cattle-raising tradition of the Hamites.

Eventually, population growth and the search for fresh grazing caused a southerly migration, as the areas to the north and west were already populated, while the few bands of Bushmen and Hottentots to the south offered little or no resistance. It is estimated that the first scattered groups of Bantu arrived in what today is South Africa about 900 years ago. The movement was not concerted and simultaneous, and various groups took different routes.

Five main groups of Bantu are distinguished today. The first, the Nguni, spread through the eastern Transvaal down the east coast. Several Nguni nations can be distinguished: of these, the Xhosa live in Transkei and Ciskei, the Zulu in Zululand and Natal, the Swazi in Swaziland and the Transvaal, and the Ndebele in the central Transvaal.

A second group of Bantu, the Sotho, spread westward about 500 years ago, the North Sotho (Pedi) settling in the northern and eastern Transvaal, the West Sotho (Tswana) furthest west in Botswana and adjacent areas of South Africa, and the South Sotho (Basotho) in Lesotho and the Orange Free State.

A third group, the Ovambo-Herero, went even further west, settling in what is today South-West Africa/Namibia. About 300 years ago a fourth group, the Venda, made their appearance in the northern Transvaal. Even later, in the course of the 19th century, a fifth group, the Tsonga, migrated from the Portuguese possessions on the east coast to the Transvaal.

The movements of the Bantu were checked at an imaginary line running from the Great Fish River in the east to the Orange River in the west. At this stage the Bantu had, more or less, driven the Bushmen and Hottentots into the southernmost corner of Africa, and one can assume that, then, they encountered stronger resistance. There are, in fact, indications that, at this stage, the most southerly Bantu tribes were preparing for a last assault on the south, as other tribes pressed on them from behind. The Bantu were, however, plagued by internal strife, and, instead of uniting into large units, they broke up into small, weak groups, continually fighting among themselves. As a result of this, the distribution pattern of the Bantu was still very fluid at the beginning of the 19th century, which was to be a restless and disturbed time for the Black peoples of South Africa.

The Sotho call this period the *Difaqane*, meaning "bands of marauding soldiers". The *Difaqane* was, to a large extent, caused by the emergence of the Zulu nation. Originally a small tribe in what is modern Natal, they became the united and powerful people of an empire towards the end of the 18th century, when their chieftains, Dingiswayo, and later Tshaka, began a series of wars of conquest. Many tribes were completely wiped out by these conquerors. Others fled from the Zulu armies and on the way attacked other tribes to obtain food. This led to a chain reaction of violence throughout southern Africa.

A scorned outcast becomes the Black Napoleon

Tshaka was born about 1787, the son of the Zulu chieftain Senzangakona. According to the custom of his people, he began to tend his father's sheep when he was only six years old. Enraged by the boy's failure to protect one of his sheep against the attack of a wild dog, Senzangakona banished Tshaka and his mother, Nandi, from his sight. Scorned and maltreated by the children round him for having been rejected by his father, Tshaka grew up with a burning ambition to achieve greatness.

He became the commander of one of the regiments of Dingiswayo, chief of the Mtetwa, and introduced the terrifying Zulu assegai – not a long-shafted missile like the ordinary spear, but a broad-bladed, short, stabbing weapon. When his father died in 1816, Dingiswayo helped Tshaka to become chief of the Zulu, and, on Dingiswayo's death in 1818, he also took over the chieftainship of the Mtetwa.

Tshaka has aptly been called the Black Napoleon, for he introduced an unheard-of state of military readiness, personally leading his men on many battlefields. Not only did he improve their weapons; the men were efficiently trained, as in a modern army. Tshaka developed a devastating tactic, the half-moon formation, in which battle-hardened veterans were the centre of the attack, while younger troops in the van, on the outside edges, outflanked the enemy.

In the end, Tshaka became a bloodthirsty despot. When his mother died in October 1827, he proclaimed cruel forms of mourning for the whole Zulu nation, and, as his power grew, he began to ignore completely the consultative principle of traditional tribal rule. He was assassinated in 1828 by his two half-brothers, Dingane and Mhlangane, as was his chief induna (senior adviser), Mbopa.

A proud nation is subjugated

At first Dingane was regarded by the Zulu as an enlightened and peace-loving ruler, a welcome change from the despotic Tshaka whom he had succeeded in 1828. Later, however, Dingane became equally harsh. In dealing with the Whites – British traders and missionaries, and the Voortrekkers (pioneers) who entered Natal in 1837 – he was often deceitful. On 6 February 1838 he ordered the murder of the Voortrekker leader, Piet Retief, and 107 of his followers. His impis (regiments) were then dealt a shattering blow by the Voortrekkers at the Battle of Blood River on 16 December of the same year, and his brother Mpande ousted him as chief.

Mpande remained conciliatory throughout his reign, which lasted until 1872, when he was succeeded by his son, Cetshwayo, cast in the war-like mould of Tshaka. Cetshwayo achieved a notable victory over British forces at Isandlwana in 1879. Banning Cetshwayo after he had lost the war, and dividing Zululand between 13 other chiefs did not prove to be a solution, and in the end the land of the proud Zulu was annexed as a British colony in 1887 at the insistence of the governor of the colony of Natal.

The Ndebele of Mzilikazi

A Zulu commander, Mzilikazi, was forced to flee to the Transvaal during the *Difaqane*. Initially he was one of Tshaka's best military leaders, but he

Two Blacks dressing an animal skin — a painting by F. T. I'Ons, an English artist who settled in the eastern Cape in 1834.

Scene at a Black settlement at Fort Beaufort in the north-eastern Cape in the 19th century - painting by Thomas Baines.

had ambitions of his own, and after a raid on a neighbouring tribe in 1822, he refused to hand over to Tshaka the cattle he had seized. He beat off Tshaka's punitive force, but knew that his life was no longer safe while he was within reach of the Zulu chief.

Fleeing to the Transvaal, Mzilikazi subjugated the whole area, as well as large parts of Botswana, within ten years, incorporating the young and fit Sotho in his tribe, and killing the others. By then the tribe was known as the Ndebele. Mzilikazi's despotism and his warlike nature brought him into conflict with the Voortrekkers, who were entering the Transvaal at this time. They drove him across the Limpopo River into what is now Zimbabwe and the present home of the Ndebele nation.

"The Shaver" founds a nation

Although the Southern and Northern Sotho were weak in comparison with the Zulu and the Ndebele, the Basotho (the Southern Sotho) were able to maintain themselves in the mountain fastness of what is today the kingdom of Lesotho (formerly Basutoland), defying even the might of Mzilikazi. In the end they voluntarily became British subjects in 1868. The Pedi (the Northern Sotho) fled from various upheavals as best they could, sometimes going as far as the Kalahari Desert, or else hiding in the ravines and caves of the northern Transvaal. They came under the authority of the Voortrekkers once these pioneers had defeated Mzilikazi, but one tribe, the Pedi, remained fiercely independent until the British finally subjugated their chief, Sekhukhuni, in 1880.

When a young warrior called Lepoqo, of the Bamokoteli, one of the many weak and scattered Basotho tribes, sought to distinguish himself, he did so in the traditional Bantu manner – he raided another tribe's cattle. At the feast after the successful outcome, Lepoqo was lauded as the man who had "shaved the enemy's beard". In typical onoma-

topoeic fashion, his nickname became Mosh-weshwe, its sounds resembling those made by a sharp razor as it removes the stubble of a beard.

Moshweshwe gradually gathered more and more members of the weaker tribes about him, and finally, in 1824, he settled with about 2 000 followers on Thaba Bosigo (the Mountain of the Night) in the Drakensberg range. Thaba Bosigo was a natural fortress with a flat top, excellent soil, and more than enough water. By blocking six natural points of entry with rocks in times of war, Moshweshwe could withstand virtually any period of siege, and his fortress became a welcome refuge for tribesmen persecuted by the Zulu or the Ndebele. By 1829, Moshweshwe had 5 000 followers; they called themselves the Basotho.

When Mzilikazi attacked him unsuccessfully in 1831, Moshweshwe politely sent some cattle after the departing enemy as provender, a piece of diplomacy which won him lasting exemption from further attack by the Ndebele. In later life, Moshweshwe found it difficult to control his followers, and there were clashes with both the Voortrekkers and the British colonial authorities. By a master-stroke of diplomacy, knowing that ·he would eventually be defeated, Moshweshwe succeeded in finding refuge for his nation as protectorate of the British Crown two years before his death in 1870.

The Western Sotho, or Tswana, consisted of a number of tribes plagued by internal differences. There were, among others, the Bamangwato, the Tlhaping (or "fishermen", after the staple diet which they caught in the Vaal River), and the Rolong. When the Rolong granted Voortrekker descendants some land in return for help in inter-tribal warfare, and these Whites established a small republic, the British authorities intervened by annexing Bechuanaland (now Botswana) as a protectorate on 30 September 1885.

A tribe which submitted to European authority only late in the 19th century was the Venda, who had migrated to the mountainous north-eastern Transvaal from modern Zimbabwe during the

"Peclu, son of Mateebe, King of the Bechuanas", painted by H. C. de Meillon.

previous century. The Venda knew how to mine copper. Once again, internal feuds and clashes with the Transvaal authorities finally led to the subjugation of the Venda in 1898.

The first meetings between White and Black

The Xhosa and the Pondo in the south were the tribes that bore the brunt of the contact between White and Black. White and Black first met about 1770 in the vicinity of the Great Fish River, then the eastern frontier of the Cape Colony. It was to become a scene of a series of confrontations known as the Frontier Wars. When the Whites were checked in the east, they moved inland across the Orange River, thus effectively separating the western and eastern Bantu, but laying themselves open to attack on both flanks. By curving east across the Drakensberg into Natal, the Whites then wedged themselves between the two major Nguni groups on the east coast, the Zulu and the Xhosa. However, the Great Fish River clashes were the decisive factor in the history of the Xhosa.

The Xhosa, named after one of their earliest chieftains, never succeeded in establishing a unified empire like the Zulu. Dissension is a feature of their tribal history; and by the time clashes between them and the White frontiersmen took on serious proportions, there were two major chieftains: Ngqika (Gaika), the rightful heir to the chieftainship of the Xhosa, and his uncle, Ndlambe, who had been loath to relinquish his regency when Gaika claimed his inheritance. Ndlambe and his followers then settled west of the Great Fish River.

Early clashes set a pattern of contention

The Xhosa, like the colonists, were cattle-farmers, and it was inevitable that they should start competing for grazing in the same area. In addition, White and Black never understood each other's different systems of land-ownership.

Among the Blacks, the chief "owned" the land merely as a representative. Land was, in fact, regarded as communal property to be apportioned by the chief as he saw fit, but it was never alienated from the possession of the tribe to that of an individual. This was diametrically opposed to the European system, under which an individual could obtain inalienable personal rights through a title-deed.

Inevitably this led to misunderstandings and clashes, apart from the fact that there was rapaciousness and plundering on both sides. The first attempt to establish the Great Fish River as the border was made by the Dutch governor Joachim van Plettenberg as early as 1778, but, instead of confirming this arrangement with the then paramount chief, Rharhabe, Van Plettenberg negotiated with lesser chiefs. By 1780 two punitive commandos had been sent to push the Xhosa back across the river.

The First Frontier War was, in reality, little more than a series of skirmishes; in May and June 1781 a commando under a well-known farmer, Adriaan van Jaarsveld, tried to drive the Xhosa out of the Suurveld (Sourveld), the area west of the Great Fish River. But the Xhosa soon returned. Meanwhile, some colonists had also moved across the border, this leading to the establishment of the Graaff-Reinet district under a *landdrost*, M. H. O. Woeke, in order to enforce economic and territorial separation. The economies of the VOC did not, however, allow Woeke to maintain an efficient police force, and by 1793 further hostilities had broken out. Instead of the Xhosa being brought under control, Woeke was ordered to be conciliatory, and the Second Frontier War dragged on inconclusively for a number of years.

British attempts to settle "the frontier question" fared no better. Towards the end of the first British occupation, in 1802, General Dundas patched up a hasty and ineffective armistice to end the third war.

When Sir John Cradock, the Earl of Caledon's successor as governor, took firm action during the early years of the second British occupation, in February 1812, he was reprimanded by his superiors, and indignantly tendered his resignation. In 1817 Somerset negotiated with Ngqika an agreement that the chief to whose kraal any tracks of stolen cattle led would be held responsible for their theft. Forced to assist Ngqika in his struggles with Ndlambe, Somerset provoked a large-scale retaliatory attack from the latter which even threatened Grahamstown. This fifth war resulted in the proclamation by Somerset of a neutral zone, but his efforts were frustrated by outraged philanthropists.

By December 1834 the destructive Sixth Frontier War was in full swing. Twenty-two colonists lost their lives, 456 homesteads were burnt, and several hundred thousand head of cattle were stolen. The governor, Sir Benjamin D'Urban, and Colonel (later Sir) Harry Smith ended hostilities, but the Cape Dutch were firmly convinced that they could not expect lasting protection from the British, and the Great Trek of frontier farmers from the Cape Colony began.

In 1846-1847 the Seventh Frontier War took place in the wake of the Glenelg policy (named after Lord Glenelg, the British Colonial Secretary), which was again conciliatory and was interpreted by the Xhosa as a sign of weakness. Twice more, in 1850 and 1877, there was war on the frontier for a variety of reasons, by which time the British assumed direct control over what is today Transkei. For the Xhosa, these wars meant the systematic debilitation of their political and military power, and by 1894 the British had incorporated Transkei into the Cape Colony.

Tswana women shape earthen pots, with a granary in the background. The artist is S. Daniell, an English traveller who was at the Cape from 1800 to 1806.

24

A peaceful rebellion shapes the future

Beginning in the middle thirties of the 19th century, a unique event took place. It was to determine not only the physical configuration of 20th-century South Africa, but was to be the source of social, political and cultural forces which shape South Africa to this day. In essence, it was a peaceful rebellion during which not a single shot was fired at established authority. Known as the Great Trek, it developed further in the late 1830s and early 1840s, and concluded in the mid-1850s. It was an event marked by deeds of endurance, heroism and hardship which became the stuff of legends, the bones of the mythology which forms the national consciousness of the majority of Whites in South Africa today.

Causes of the Great Trek

Although the British authorities were opposed to expanding the Cape Colony further to the north after 1824, they were compelled to move the frontier to the Kareeberg range, the Orange River and the Stormberg Spruit, since they wished to keep most of the *trekboers* within the colony. Yet many of them were settling or making regular visits in search of grazing well beyond the bounds of the Cape Colony. By the time the idea of the Great Trek – in effect a large-scale emigration from the Cape Colony – had come to full flower, it was abundantly clear that the Voortrekkers had no intention of returning to the Cape, while maintaining strong social and trading ties with the mother colony.

The direct causes of the Great Trek were diffuse, but it cannot be seen as an extension of the *trekboer* movement, which had served chiefly to provide the Afrikaner with physical and psychological mobility and self-reliance. Neither was any desire for conquest one of its causes, although the inevitable confrontations between the Voortrekkers and the Blacks were to be seen in this light by future Black historians. The decision to abandon British rule can largely be found in the widespread dissatisfaction of the Afrikaner on the frontier. He had been severely affected by the emancipation of the slaves, and regulations inspired by philanthropism had weakened his control over his non-White labourers. He had repeatedly suffered ruinous losses from the wars and thefts on the border, and in 1838 one farmer said that the Xhosa "came and robbed me of everything, as was the case in 1819 and again in 1834. What have I left after many years of striving and hard work? Literally nothing!" Yet, due partly to the prevailing British policy of economies, and partly to philanthropic propaganda, the frontier farmers received little or no direct government protection, no support for the commando system, no compensation for losses, and no relief from taxation.

Grievances were not confined to material matters only, but extended to two further aspects of British policy: equality between White and non-White, and lack of self-government for Whites. Afrikaners based their attitude to non-Whites on three distinctions: the difference between the Christian White and the heathen non-White; the physical differences between the European and the indigenous races; and the difference between their respective positions in the existing social structure. There could, therefore, be no equality between "us" and "them". Where, in the days of VOC rule, there had been limited local self-government in the form of the *landdrost* and *heemraden*, their posts disappeared when the British policy of highly centralized

The most important routes taken by the Voortrekkers from the Cape Colony to the areas north and east of the Orange River.

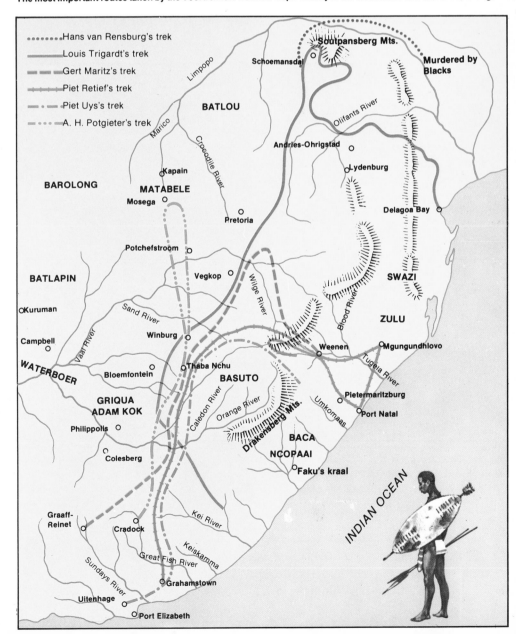

Legend:
- Hans van Rensburg's trek
- Louis Trigardt's trek
- Gert Maritz's trek
- Piet Retief's trek
- Piet Uys's trek
- A. H. Potgieter's trek

rule was introduced. Consequently, many decisions closely affecting frontier farmers were applied without consultation. Not unnaturally, this led to deep resentment. Among other causes of resentment was the policy of Anglicization.

All these factors interacted to convince the Afrikaner that the situation had become intolerable. The ingenious solution of simply leaving the area was a peaceful rebellion which embarrassed the British, who hesitated for so long before taking any action that the Voortrekkers were able to overcome their initial·difficulties and establish themselves firmly in their new territories.

Relatively few Whites supported the Great Trek, although there was widespread discontent throughout the colony. The British settlers on the eastern frontier – although on the whole sympathetic to the Voortrekkers – did not join them, probably because they did not have the *trekboer* self-reliance. The discontented Afrikaners in the western districts (with the exception of Swellendam), and towards the north, remained in the colony, mainly because they had never been subjected to the sort of debilitation caused by the frontier wars. Consequently, most of the Voortrekkers came from the eastern frontier districts, and, up to 1840, the estimated number of emigrants from the affected territory was not more than 20 per cent of the White inhabitants, and probably only about nine per cent of the total White population of the colony. Altogether about 6 000 people trekked into the interior.

Start of the Great Trek

Considerable organizational difficulties had to be overcome by the leaders of the Great Trek. They had to resolve serious differences of opinion about where to go and, at the same time, had to keep arrangements secret from the British authorities. At the end of the Trek there beckoned the material benefit of abundant fertile land in areas depopulated by Black intertribal strife, and the ideal of a free and independent Afrikaner state. As preparations were secret, it can only be assumed that those who led the vanguard were the chief planners of the Trek.

Louis Trigardt (Trichardt) and Hans van Rensburg, fearless but impetuous pioneers, emigrated in 1835, opening up the Transvaal Lowveld and the Portuguese east coast; Andries Hendrik Potgieter, the constructive founder of a settlement in the far north, left at the end of 1835 or early in 1836; Gert Maritz, inclined to be irascible, but a gifted administrator, trekked in September 1836, and it is known that he was active in making the preparatory arrangements. In September 1834 Piet Uys, of Uitenhage, had already led an exploratory party along the coastal route to Natal, declaring it an acceptable area on his return early in 1835. Further scouting expeditions went as far as the Soutpansberg range in the northern Transvaal and even to South-West Africa/Namibia.

The attitudes of the British authorities to frontier conditions were widely divergent, and their initial reactions indecisive and, on the whole, futile. Thus, the earliest Voortrekkers became more and more confident about their ability to cross the Cape frontier with arms and ammunition in defiance of colonial laws, and their movement gained considerable impetus when a respected community leader, Piet Retief of Grahamstown, decided that he, too, would join them. On the eve of his departure he published a manifesto on the establishment of an independent Voortrekker state, saying: "We quit this colony under the full assurance that the English government has nothing more to require of us, and will allow us to govern ourselves without its interference in future." The manifesto was published in *The Graham's Town Journal* on 2 February 1837, as was a list of 366 new Voortrekkers.

Retief's arrival in April 1837 in an area near Thaba 'Nchu, where a few thousand Voortrekkers had already chosen a provisional government, was none too soon, for there was considerable friction between the two recognized leaders, Gert Maritz and Andries Potgieter, particularly over the ultimate destination of the Trek. Retief was elected "chief leader", with the title of governor, and succeeded, largely, in reconciling Maritz and Potgieter. In October of the previous year Potgieter had successfully withstood an Ndebele attack under Mzilikazi at the Battle of Vegkop, and subsequent punitive expeditions which included Maritz and Uys finally broke the power of the Ndebele in November 1837.

THE WORLD AT LARGE

1836 Texas declares itself independent of Mexico and proclaims a republican constitution.
1840 Napoleon's remains are brought from St Helena to Les Invalides in Paris.
1844 In Britain the Factory Act restricts women workers to a 12-hour day, and children between 8 and 13 to 6½ hours.
1850 The Australian Government Act grants representative government to South Australia, Tasmania and Victoria.
1855 In November the missionary David Livingstone becomes the first White man to set eyes on the Victoria Falls (the Zambezi River).

Departure from the frontier districts on a long an arduous journey into an unknown interior.

A contemporary drawing of Dingane in dancing dress which was first published in London in 1836.

THE TREK DEALT A SERIOUS BLOW

When Retief and his party arrived at Mgungundhlovu on 3 February 1838, they camped outside the kraal and impressed Dingane with a mock battle, while his impi performed a war-dance, and the cattle were returned. The following day was devoted to negotiations and the drafting of the treaty, and yet another to warlike celebrations during which an ugly mood developed, but was ignored by Retief and his men.

On 6 February the Voortrekkers were specifically asked to leave their arms outside the kraal when they appeared before Dingane for a final signing which was soon concluded. More war-dances followed, the impi moving more and more closely to the Voortrekker party, until Dingane shouted: *"Bulalani abatagati!"* ("Kill the wizards!") The whole party was overwhelmed within minutes, bound with rawhide thongs, and clubbed to death outside the kraal. Dingane's treachery was caused mainly by his fear of the military strength of the Voortrekkers, a fear that was doubtless inflamed by his advisers. After the attack on Retief, Dingane immediately dispatched his impis, during the night, to overwhelm the Voortrekker encampments (called **laagers**) on the Upper Tugela River. The Great Trek was in dire danger.

Potgieter still wanted to settle in the north, now the Transvaal, for the Ndebele had been defeated and had fled across the Limpopo River. But finally he joined the majority under Retief and Maritz, who had decided that Natal was their destination. A factor which probably influenced Potgieter's decision was that it was known by then that Van Rensburg and his entire party had lost their lives in an attack in mid-1836 near the Limpopo. (Trigardt and his trek were to struggle down to the Portuguese at Delagoa Bay, where all but 25 of the party finally succumbed to malaria, a danger in this tropical area from the outset.)

Overcoming considerable difficulties, Retief's party arrived at Port Natal (Durban) on, probably, 20 October 1837. They were welcomed as future neighbours by most of the British settlers there; one of them, Alexander Biggar, emphasized that a Voortrekker state would safeguard them against Dingane, and consequently promote trade. Retief succeeded in obtaining an assurance from Dingane that he and his followers would be granted an extensive area between the Tugela (Thukela) and Mzimvubu rivers if they recovered cattle stolen from Dingane by the Tlokwa chieftain Sikonyella – a raid which Dingane wrongly suspected had been carried out by the Voortrekkers. Retief returned to his main party in northern Natal, where there was still dissension because of administrative arrangements he had introduced, and was forced to act quickly so as to complete his negotiations with Dingane, and thus justify his policy. He recovered the cattle from Sikonyella, and, despite warnings about the untrustworthiness of Dingane, returned to the chief's main kraal at Mgungundhlovu on 25 January 1838 with 70 Voortrekkers, an English interpreter, and 30 Cape Coloured followers. On 6 February, after Dingane had signed the treaty drafted by Retief, this unarmed party was overwhelmed and killed at Dingane's command.

Dingane's impis struck quickly at *laagers* on the Bushmans and Bloukrans rivers, where about 300 Voortrekkers and more than 200 non-White servants lost their lives. The remainder regrouped at a *laager* called Doornkloof, and sent for help across the Drakensberg to the Orange Free State. Meanwhile, Potgieter and Piet Uys had returned from their final punitive expedition against Mzilikazi, and it was agreed that Dingane was to be attacked. The headstrong Voortrekkers, however, could not agree on a single leader. The result was that Potgieter and Uys were appointed military commanders, with equal status, while Maritz remained at the *laager* as head of the government. Consisting of 347 mounted men and a few Coloured people and pack animals, the divided commando left Doornkloof on 6 April 1838. The result was a lamentable failure. At the Battle of Italeni the Zulu not only had the upper hand tactically, but succeeded in ambushing Uys and his commando as a result of the independent tactics of each leader.

A boy hero's death

Initially the Uys commando put to flight the "White Shield" impi, while Potgieter was preparing to attack the "Black Shields". During the pursuit Uys's men scattered dangerously, and were in no position to counter an attack by a third Zulu force in reserve, which had remained in hiding.

Uys was wounded in the left hip by an assegai, and his men fled. He ordered two men who were supporting him to leave and save their own lives, an order which his 12-year-old son, Dirkie, also obeyed. But, turning back and seeing his father at the mercy of the advancing Zulu, Dirkie came to his aid. He and his father died together under the Zulu spears.

Potgieter's commando had been more careful. But only about 18 of his men fired a volley at the Zulu, and all of them were put to flight by the "Black Shields". Some Uys survivors managed to join them, and there were bitter recriminations in the Voortrekker camp. Potgieter and his followers left to seek their fortunes in the north, where he had always wanted to go and where, between the Vet and the Vaal rivers, he obtained land in exchange for cattle.

Some of the Voortrekkers under the leadership of Karel Landman retreated to Port Natal. Others spent an uneasy winter in their fortified *laagers* in

the Tugela valley. When Gert Maritz died on 23 September 1838, the Voortrekkers were leaderless. They turned to Andries Pretorius, a Graaff-Reinet man whom they knew well. A gifted organizer and military leader, Pretorius probably made the most constructive individual contribution to the Great Trek, once he had decided to identify himself with the movement. He was appointed commandant-general on 25 November, and immediately prepared to counter-attack Dingane's forces. His victory at the Battle of Blood River was the decisive event of the Great Trek.

A short-lived republic

The first Voortrekker republic, with a *volksraad* (House of Representatives) as its highest governmental body, was then founded. It did not last long, but was constantly under direct and indirect pres-

A SOLEMN VOW SHAPES THE CONSCIENCE OF A NATION

On 15 December 1838 Pretorius gathered his forces in a well-fortified *laager*, strategically placed between a deep section of a tributary of the Buffalo River and a large ditch. It could be attacked from one side only. With Pretorius were about 470 men, confronted by about 12 500 Zulu, who, relying on their numerical superiority, launched a series of frontal attacks on the *laager*. They were beaten back by devastating Voortrekker gunfire and two small cannon which Pretorius had brought with him.

Some days before the battle (after which the Buffalo was renamed "Blood River" because of the crushing Zulu losses), the Voortrekkers had vowed that, if God granted them victory, they and their descendants would always remember the day and would build a church in honour of the Lord. This vow inspired the Voortrekkers in one of the biggest and most decisive battles ever fought between Black and White in South Africa, a battle in which more than 3 000 Zulu lost their lives. The annual commemoration of the vow created an Afrikaner tradition which endures to this day.

The Voortrekker Monument, inaugurated in 1949, is richly endowed with symbolism derived from the Great Trek.

sure from British authorities who would not recognize its independence and who wanted to see its territory under British rule. Taking into consideration its sparse population and its relative administrative inexperience, the republic fared reasonably well. It even achieved a union with Potgieter further north. During 1841, the British, however, found sufficient justification for bringing Natal to heel. The *volksraad* was moving thousands of unsettled Blacks to the southern boundary of Natal. This the governor of the Cape, Sir George Napier, thought would lead to dangerous pressures on his own eastern frontier. Napier dispatched Captain T. C. Smith to Port Natal, and he established a British presence there in May 1842, fought the Voortrekkers unsuccessfully at Congella, and was besieged by Pretorius. The siege ended after a British settler, Dick King, rode 600 miles to Grahamstown – an astonishing achievement – and obtained reinforcements. The *volksraad* signed the terms of capitulation at Pietermaritzburg on 15 July 1842.

For more or less the same reasons behind the Great Trek, a second trek then gathered momentum more militantly, as settlers left to join the Afrikaners in the north and in the area between the Orange and the Vaal rivers. This time, however, the British were determined to control the trekkers. Matters came to a head in February 1848, when Sir Harry Smith, then the governor at the Cape, annexed the whole of the territory between the Orange and the Vaal rivers and the Drakensberg, and created the Orange River Sovereignty. Potgieter's people were fairly firmly established at various centres beyond the Vaal (now the Transvaal). An attempt made by Pretorius, also in the Transvaal, to dislodge Smith was heavily defeated at Boomplaats in August 1848.

But the British government had bitten off more than it could chew. Its financial commitments had increased. It could not police its vastly extended territories; the Eighth Frontier War was taking its toll; and Moshweshwe and his Basotho were troublesome. In addition, there was the possibility that the self-governing Transvalers might interfere in the affairs of the Orange River Sovereignty on behalf of their compatriots. Policy in Britain shifted towards the conviction that it would be better to make allies of Voortrekkers who could then be relied on to help to protect Britain's extensive frontiers in southern Africa. Thus, while Potgieter isolated himself ever more, and bitterly disapproved of Pretorius's attitude, the latter came to negotiate

Andries Pretorius, who led the Voortrekkers in their decisive battle against Dingane's Zulu.

with the British at Sand River, in the northern part of the Sovereignty.

On 17 January 1852 the Convention of Sand River brought about the first British recognition of a Voortrekker republic, the community north of the Vaal. Even Potgieter came to accept this, solemnly accepting reconciliation with Pretorius at Rustenburg with a handshake over an open Bible.

In March 1853 the British government informed its high commissioner at the Cape, Cathcart, that he should try to establish a second buffer state in the Orange River Sovereignty. Despite the opposition of English-speaking people there, Cathcart's special commissioner, Sir George Clerk, forced the issue, and the Bloemfontein Convention was signed on 23 February 1854. For the first time the British flag was lowered in an annexed territory in southern Africa. Two Voortrekker republics were in existence, this being the logical conclusion of the Great Trek.

These republics were not the only significant result of the Trek. While the republics were to have their share of governmental problems because of their democratic freedom, Britain lost its finest opportunity of retaining firm control of southern Africa. While the fortunes of Briton and Boer in South Africa were to fluctuate well into the 20th century, the Boer had, in fact, gained the ascendancy. His national consciousness and identity had been given a nurturing ground during this, his first heroic epoch. He had succeeded relatively bloodlessly in seizing his own freedom and, despite future reversals, was never to abandon the republican ideal. A negative result was the first serious estrangement between British and Afrikaners – the two main White allies in a Black continent. And there were still many problems. The Voortrekkers had no port of their own; confrontations with Black people had extended over a much wider area; and economic conditions were barely above the subsistence level.

British colonies and Boer republics

Canada had been given a form of representative self-government in 1840, as had the Australian states in 1850, and by this time the British were also more sympathetic to the idea of self-government at the Cape. In 1846 London asked Sir Harry Smith for a report on the matter, and William Porter, attorney-general at the time, drew up proposals which were forwarded to Britain in March 1848. By December 1852 Porter had drawn up a draft constitution which was ratified by Britain after revisions of the franchise qualifications. The new constitution took effect on 1 July 1853 and, apart from a few amendments, remained in force until 1910.

There was to be a legislative council or upper house, consisting of the chief justice (as president) and 15 elected members, and a legislative assembly of 46 elected members. The franchise was given to all male British subjects over 21, regardless of race, colour or religion, if they had not been found guilty of certain specified crimes, and if they lived in a building worth £25, or earned at least £50 a year. In theory, Coloured persons and Blacks could qualify for the franchise and put themselves forward as candidates. The language of the debates was to be English.

The executive consisted of the governor, who was the only person empowered to introduce financial measures in the lower house, and his officials, who had no vote but attended sessions as heads of departments and were responsible solely to the governor. There was thus no cabinet and, in fact, legislation was largely subject to the wishes of the governor. This was hardly an ideal structure; that there were no serious conflicts between legislative and executive authorities in the early years must be ascribed largely to the tact of the governor, Sir George Grey.

Grey, a man with a military background, had been appointed governor of South Australia in 1841, and there he had revived the young colony's economy, which had been tottering on the verge of bankruptcy. In 1845 he became governor of New Zealand, where his able handling of the Maori problem in particular had been applauded. On his arrival in South Africa, Grey was particularly anxious to establish firm British authority over the Xhosa on the border of the Cape Colony. This he tried to do by integrating them into the economy, instead of following the traditional policy of territorial separation. It irked Grey that this was, by and large, the policy followed in the two Boer republics, and he did what he could to establish a common Black policy throughout southern Africa.

The ideal of a greater South Africa

Eventually, Grey's Xhosa policy proved unsuccessful, and these territories were incorporated into the Cape Colony. In pursuing his efforts to establish a uniform Black policy throughout southern Africa, and also to place the region on a firmer economic footing, Grey envisaged a greater, unified South Africa. It did not suit him that there was a move north of the Orange River to unify the two Voortrekker republics – the Orange Free State and Transvaal – since this would hamper his efforts. He therefore proposed a federation between the Cape and the Orange Free State. This proposal fell on receptive ears, as the Free State was having trouble with the Basotho. After hearing from the Free State *volksraad* that it would co-operate, Grey raised the matter in the Cape parliament in March 1859. But the British government, enraged at this and other arbitrary actions for which Grey had no authority, immediately recalled him. He was reinstated only briefly and then again became governor of New Zealand.

Apart from commerce and trade, there was little further contact between the two British colonies and the two Boer republics. The Cape steadily developed its agriculture, its roads and railways, its local government and its educational facilities. The main conflicts were constitutional, especially after Grey had been succeeded by Sir Philip Wodehouse (1862-1870). Wodehouse was autocratic and high-handed, hostile to any form of self-government. He disapproved of a movement in the eastern Cape which advocated secession for this area from the western Cape. To make matters worse for him, there was a world-wide recession, and a lengthy drought which increased the colony's debts and led to higher taxation. Wodehouse was hardly popular.

He also succeeded in alienating the Orange Free State, when, in 1868, at the request of Moshweshwe, he annexed Basutoland, just when Moshweshwe was about to be punished, once and for all, for alleged aggressions. Wodehouse's financial measures and his reversion to autocracy at every opportunity produced a constitutional deadlock, and he was replaced in 1870 by Sir Henry Barkly.

Barkly was a passionate advocate of self-government as a means of reducing the burden of the British taxpayer and as a basis for federation with the other territories in South Africa. Although the

The epic ride of Dick King from Durban to Grahamstown brought relief to besieged British forces – and a reward of £15.

A DESPERATE RIDE BRINGS UNDYING FAME

In 1842, when Captain T. C. Smith's forces were defeated by the Voortrekkers at Congella, the future of Natal hung in the balance. The issue was decided by Richard Philip (Dick) King, who, in 1820, had arrived at the Cape as an eight-year-old boy with British settler parents who went to Natal about eight years later.

King had come to know the wild coast between Port Natal and Grahamstown, for he transported goods to and fro by wagon. He agreed to raise the alarm and obtain a relief force. Escaping across the bay by boat on 26 May with a trusted Zulu servant, Ndongeni, Dick King rode 960 km in 10 days through inhospitable country and past hostile tribes. On his arrival on his horse, Somerset, reinforcements were dispatched immediately. King's reward was £15. His was a ride which won the admiration of friend and foe alike.

Peaceful development of the Cape Colony brought restful prosperity to Cape Town, painted here about 1850 by W. H. F. Langschmidt.

scarcely alleviated by the institution of a legislative council in 1848 which had the right to pass laws where there was urgency. Only on 24 March 1857 did a constitution provide for a legislative council of four officials and twelve elected members, after the colony had been separated from the Cape the previous year. Because of rapid economic and population growth, the Natalians began, in the 1880s, to demand a more representative form of government, and this was finally introduced in 1893, when a bicameral parliament came into being.

One of the young colony's major problems was the thousands of Black vagrants who roamed the countryside, stealing cattle and squatting on White-owned land. On 31 March 1846, the first governor of Natal, Martin West, appointed a commission to consider the matter, and there resulted the location or reserve policy, which attempted the permanent settlement of Blacks in designated areas. Initially the policy was neither successful nor popular. The farmers felt that they were being deprived of labour or of land earmarked for the reserves, and a number of trekkers still living in Natal decided to leave. The supervision of the locations was also inadequate. West's successor, Benjamin Pine, reconsidered the problem in 1852, and one of the members of the legislative council, Theophilus Shepstone, who had hitherto been diplomatic agent for the Natives, as the Blacks were then called, was appointed Secretary for Native Affairs. Largely because of his tactful control, which maintained the Blacks within the framework of traditional tribal ties, the location policy began to succeed. But there were two serious clashes between the Natal authorities and the Blacks. In 1873 the Hlubi chief, Langalibalele, refused to register the guns obtained by his tribesmen. A punitive expedition was sent out, and he was exiled to Robben Island, Table Bay. In 1879, Cetshwayo's Zulu became belligerent, and inflicted heavy losses on the British at Isandlwana before being defeated at the Battle of Ulundi on 4 July 1879. Cetshwayo was also sent to Cape Town in exile.

In its early years the colony of Natal eked out a precarious economic existence. Agriculture de-

parliamentarian John Charles Molteno had his approval for the introduction of a motion requesting self-government (a motion which had failed in 1860), it failed again in 1871. The following year it was carried by only a single vote, Molteno becoming the first prime minister on 1 December. Henceforth the governor was only the representative of the British government, and high commissioner for British territories in southern Africa.

The Cape Afrikaners had gradually lost their enthusiasm for public affairs, but about 1870 there was a clear resurgence of Afrikaner nationalism. It found expression in the formation of the Association of True Afrikaners at Paarl in 1875, the objective of which was "championing our language, our nation and our country". After Britain had annexed the Transvaal in 1877, J. H. Hofmeyr became the leader of the Afrikaner Bond, a political party which was to play an important part in the history of the colony.

Steady development in Natal

In Britain's other colony in southern Africa, Natal, the Afrikaner played virtually no role. After annexation the *volksraad* of the short-lived Voortrekker republic continued to exist until 1845, but many Afrikaners had left on their second trek. Natal became a district of the Cape Colony on 31 May

1844, but proper British rule over the area was instituted only in December 1845. The government had an executive (a lieutenant-governor assisted by a council of five members) but all legislative authority was vested in the government of the Cape Colony.

This was not a practical state of affairs, one

THE WORLD AT LARGE

1850 Clayton-Bulwer Agreement between Britain and the United States not to seek exclusive control of a proposed Panama Canal.
1857 Birth of Robert Baden-Powell, defender of Mafeking and founder of the world-wide Boy Scout movement.
1865 Assassination of Abraham Lincoln by John Wilkes Booth.
1872 The Royal Albert Hall opened in London.

The ox-wagon was the Cape Colony's trade vehicle for a long time, although road and rail links were improved considerably towards the second half of the 19th century. In this painting by E. J. Austen (c. 1880) wagons are crossing a river at night.

A NATION COMMITS SUICIDE

Grey's policy of civilizing through economic measures led to fierce resistance from the Xhosa, resistance that was exploited by one of their leaders, Kreli. Through a young girl, Nonquase, and her uncle, a witchdoctor called Umhlakaza, Kreli spread the rumour that ancestral spirits were demanding that the Xhosa should destroy their cattle and provisions. On 18 February 1857, it was said, all their dead heroes and the food would rise out of the earth, and the White intruders would be blown into the sea. Perhaps Kreli hoped that his followers would then make a hysterical mass attack across the border and destroy the White government once and for all.

The resulting famine was a major tragedy. Tens of thousands of people died, and about 30 000 streamed across the border in search of food and work. But this national suicide gave Grey the opportunity of settling depopulated areas with about 2 300 ex-servicemen of the Crimean War, as well as 4 000 German settlers obtained through a recruiting firm in Hamburg.

clined because of the exodus of the Voortrekkers, there were few roads, and the British government gave little financial aid. However, as the population increased, chiefly because immigration was encouraged, matters improved. Cotton and coffee were planted experimentally, but the greatest success was sugar. By 1872 there were about 2 500 hectares under cane, and 83 factories were producing almost 9 000 tons of sugar. The population had increased from an estimated 2 000 Whites and 100 000 Blacks in the 1840s to 22 000 and more than 300 000 respectively in 1878.

The Natal government actively strengthened trade ties with the Cape Colony and the two Boer republics, and by 1892 all three had rail links with Natal. Natal also extended its borders. In 1845 the British had declared that the frontiers were the Tugela and Buffalo rivers in the north, the Drakensberg in the west, and the Mzimkulu river in the south. (In the east was the Indian Ocean.) In 1866, however, part of Pondoland, in the south, was incorporated, and in 1897 Zululand was absorbed. These acquisitions virtually doubled the size of Natal.

Culturally, Natal developed along purely British lines, and even today is still whimsically referred to as "the last outpost of the British Empire". At one stage, no less than six newspapers were appearing in the colony (two of which still survive), and Natal, unlike the three other territories, developed and maintained the strong British identity which it has never lost.

A shaky start for the Orange Free State

Naturally, the Boer or Afrikaner tradition was dominant in both republics from the outset. The word "Boer" at first meant nothing more than "farmer". At the Cape, it was applied to the Dutch in a derogatory way, although it has retained its original meaning to this day. Like their Dutch forefathers, who responded to the derogatory epithet *Watergeuse* ("Beggars of the sea", which they were

called in the war with Spain) by converting it into an accolade, the Afrikaner was and is proud to be called a Boer.

Proud the Free State Boers may have been when they achieved their independence through the Bloemfontein Convention on 23 February 1854, but their country was pitifully poor and ill-equipped for its venture into freedom. There were only about 10 000 Whites, divided by lingering loyalty to Britain or loyalty to their new republic. There were very few professional men who could be counted on to administer a government; there were continual clashes with Moshweshwe and his Basotho; and there was not even a constitution. The task of drawing up one was entrusted to an acting president, Josias Philippus Hoffman, and 29 "people's representatives". Aided by three foreigners (J. J. Groenendaal, J. M. Orpen and A. Coqui), and using the French constitution of 1848 and some clauses of the United States constitution as a model, this group of unsophisticated Boers, for many years deprived of regular schooling and inexperienced in constitutional matters, succeeded in fully expressing all the democratic and republican beliefs of the Afrikaners. They did so in less than a month.

Hoffman became state president, and Groenendaal government secretary; they were assisted by an executive committee. Legislative powers were vested in a *volksraad* of elected members to whom the state president was responsible. Justice was administered according to Roman-Dutch law. Hoffman's presidency, despite signs of achievement, lasted only a year. His resistance to the first attempts made by M. W. Pretorius, president of the Transvaal, to unite the two republics, and his conciliatory attitude to the British soon alienated the Free State republicans. When Hoffman presented a keg of gunpowder to Moshweshwe, with whom he was on friendly terms – the hope that he would be able to establish lasting peace with the Basotho had given him his position in the first place – this incident was used as a pretext to get rid of him: he

was said to have endangered the safety of the State.

The second president, Johannes Nicolaas Boshoff, was abler and more tactful, and succeeded particularly in improving the civil service. The Free State flag and coat of arms were also introduced during his term of office (1855-1859). He, too, lost the confidence of his people when he resisted unification attempts by Pretorius, but favourably considered a federation with the Cape Colony – a plan which was wrecked when Sir George Grey was recalled. Boshoff's major problem was the Basotho, whose depredations on the frontier had become intolerable. After, in 1858, declaring a war which ended in an unsatisfactory armistice, Boshoff was forced to resign in 1859.

Pretorius was then elected president of the Orange Free State as well, but he was forced to relinquish his Transvaal presidency six months later. While the Free State was largely in favour of union with the Transvaal, it feared that such a step would nullify the Sand River Convention, which guaranteed its independence, and once again the idea was rejected. Economically, the Free State slowly gained ground despite its problems. The community, mainly agricultural, was even able to withstand the worst droughts in living memory in 1860 and 1862, as well as destructive floods and hail-storms in certain areas. With an influx, largely, of British and Dutch immigrants, towns grew steadily, but, with government finance critical in 1863, Pretorius was forced to resign.

"The model republic"

The man who became president on 2 February 1864 was Johannes Hendricus Brand, a barrister and politician from the western Cape. By common consent, Brand was a statesman of extraordinary stature who, eventually, was internationally recognized and honoured by Britain and other nations. He had a towering personality, indomitable drive, and a firm sense of justice. Under his fatherly guid-

This excellent drawing by Heinrich Egersdörfer, a South African artist of German birth, shows a Boer commando on the march, with the ox-waggons carrying supplies trailing behind. The simple apparel worn by the men contrasts sharply with the gorgeous uniforms of the British Tommies against whom they fought and gained fame at Amajuba and in many another battle.

The Moravian mission at Genadendal towards the middle of the 19th century, based on a painting by G. F. Angas. Genadendal was one of many settlements founded by German, French, British and Dutch missionaries to convert the indigenous peoples to Christianity, and to introduce them to Western values.

ance, which lasted until his death on 14 July 1888, the Orange Free State came to be regarded as "the model republic".

Influential citizens of the Orange Free State asked Brand to stand for election, and his tasks, after he had won with an overwhelming majority, had been well defined. He had to put an end to hostilities with the Basotho in the east once and for all; he had to improve administration in almost every respect.

Dutch and British training produces a president

J. H. (Jan) Brand was born in Cape Town on 6 December 1823, when Lord Charles Somerset was still governor. His father was an advocate who supported both the democratic rights of the colonists and the Great Trek. Young Brand grew up in a home which, with strong Afrikaner traditions, was in predominantly English surroundings.

In 1843 Brand left South Africa to study law at the University of Leyden. Then, with a degree two years later, he was admitted to the Inner Temple, London, and became a barrister. Four years later he returned to the Cape to practise, and to become a member of the first Cape parliament in 1854. He also became part-time professor of law at the South African Athenaeum.

When he was president of the Orange Free State, one of Brand's most famous aphorisms became a permanent part of proverbial Afrikaans. "Everything will turn out well," he said, "if everyone does his duty."

With his legal training, Brand knew that written agreements were binding, and he therefore had the border between the Free State and Moshweshwe's territory determined, and saw to it that that border was confirmed by the signature of the Basotho chief. When this agreement was violated on two occasions, in 1865 and 1867, Brand did not hesitate to declare war. His encouragement of the Free State burghers led to victory on both occasions, and Moshweshwe warded off a final, annihilating blow only by obtaining the protection of the British Crown.

From 1870 onwards, Brand concentrated on developing the republic internally. After the discovery of diamonds, discussed in the following chapter, the financial position of the Free State improved considerably, and Brand ensured that the money was wisely spent. Administration was improved, and he personally supervised the

appointment of able civil servants. He laid the foundations of a better educational system with the passing of the Education Act in 1872, and in the same year instituted a Court of Appeal. Three years later he created an independent Supreme Court. He encouraged the development of trade, and by 1874 the Free State had telegraphic links with the Cape and Natal. Not only was the State greatly strengthened internally, but its independence was recognized by foreign powers. In the United States and in Europe, the Orange Free State had its own consular representatives. Brand strongly supported cordial co-operation between the states and colonies of southern Africa, but insisted on the independence of the Free State. Only in this way, he felt, could his republic compete politically and economically with its neighbours.

The Transvaal's stormy passage

Compared with its southern counterpart, the Transvaal republic had to endure a much stormier passage. At its inception under the Sand River Convention of 17 January 1852, a convention backed and signed by the old Voortrekker leader Andries Pretorius, there were at least three independent little states north of the Vaal River, one of them established by Potgieter. On the death of Pretorius on 23 July 1853, his son, Marthinus Wessel Pretorius, continued the efforts to unite independent Afrikaners north of the Vaal into one state, and, on 6 January 1857, he was sworn in as the first president of the *Zuid-Afrikaansche Republiek* (the South African Republic), its constitution having been drafted by a Dutchman, Jacobus Stuart. Although the famous Transvaal *Vierkleur* (the four-coloured flag) was hoisted for the first time on this occasion, the republic was properly unified only in 1860. This was also the year which saw the resignation of Pretorius, then

The climax of the Transvaal's First War of Independence (1880-1881) occurred at Amajuba, where British invading the Transvaal under General Sir George Pomeroy Colley were dealt a crushing blow by Boer forces under Commandant-General Piet Joubert.

also president of the Orange Free State, because of controversy over the unification of the two republics, an ideal which he had always pursued.

The resignation of Pretorius was followed by a period of internal strife which included a small-scale civil war, until Pretorius once again became president in 1864. He relinquished his ideal, and concentrated on obtaining a sea-port for the Transvaal. Thwarted in his territorial aspirations by vehement protests from the British and Portuguese, he managed to conclude a favourable trade-treaty with the latter at Delagoa Bay in 1869. In November 1871 he was again forced to resign, this time because the *volksraad* had been bitterly disappointed by the Transvaal's loss, through his dilatoriness, of its unassailable right to certain parts of the newly-discovered diamond-fields.

The Transvaal was now determined to have an "educated" president and in 1872, on the advice of Brand, it chose the Reverend Thomas François Burgers, from the Cape. He was competent, energetic, idealistic and eager to solve the republic's problems, but his very eagerness led to an over-hasty programme of reform, as well as the possi-

bility of so strengthening the Transvaal that the British would intervene. Internally, Burgers concentrated on improving the civil service and education, but resistance followed when he quite unnecessarily changed the republic's flag and coat of arms, while, in many quarters, his education policy was regarded as too liberal. Externally, Burgers considered that a rail link with Delagoa Bay was a priority for the development of the mineral-rich Transvaal, but he had become so unpopular that some of its citizens would not pay the special taxes required for the financing of the railway, while others refused to go on commando when the Pedi chief, Sekhukhuni, became troublesome in 1876.

In 1875, Burgers left on an unsuccessful mission to European bankers to raise funds for a railway to Delagoa Bay – unsuccessful chiefly because the project ran counter to the policy of the then British Secretary of State for the Colonies, Lord Carnarvon. Carnarvon regarded a federated southern Africa as advantageous for Britain, while the discovery of diamonds and also small quantities of gold had excited British interest in the interior. A

strong and independent Transvaal with its own link to the outside world did not suit Lord Carnarvon. He called on Sir Theophilus Shepstone to act (thus, incidentally, forestalling an election which Burgers would probably have lost). Shepstone arrived in Pretoria, the capital named after Andries Pretorius, on 22 January 1877, with a commission to annex the Transvaal for Britain. At first persuasively and then bluntly, he did so, and on 12 April

SOUTH AFRICA'S FIRST GOLD COIN CAUSES DISSENSION

In 1874 President Burgers ordered the minting of the first gold coin ever struck for a government in southern Africa. True to tradition, it bore his image as president, and this greatly irritated the democratic and republican Boers, so adding to his unpopularity. Only 837 coins were struck, and the *Burgerspond* today is a numismatic rarity, worth as much as R15 000.

the Union Jack was hoisted in the capital of the South African Republic.

The executive council adopted a conciliatory policy, although it could easily have bundled Shepstone's puny force of 25 policemen and eight officials out of the territory. In all, two deputations were sent to Britain to present the case of the republic. These deputations were led by Paul Kruger, who by this time had already made his mark both in politics and in the wars against Black tribes. Negotiations with Shepstone and his successor, Sir Owen Lanyon, also took place. While the Transvaal agreed that it was economically weak and that its relations with the Blacks within its borders were unsettled, it did not regard as justified the loss of its freedom to ensure the security of the British colonies, this being the argument of the British commissioners.

By the end of 1880 patience in the Transvaal had run out, and an insignificant incident ignited the powder keg. Piet Bezuidenhout's wagon was attached when he refused to pay the costs of his summons in a tax matter. The wagon was seized by Boers and returned to Bezuidenhout on the day it

was to be auctioned. This was an act of open defiance which Lanyon was powerless to prevent, and by 16 December 1880 the Boers had met at Paardekraal in a mass demonstration, at which they elected a triumvirate government consisting of Kruger, Commandant-General Piet Joubert and M. W. Pretorius, while the *Vierkleur* was hoisted at Heidelberg, the seat of the provisional government.

Hostilities broke out at Potchefstroom on the same day, and the Transvaal Republic's First War of Independence began with sporadic skirmishes in various other places. The first pitched battle took place at Bronkhorstspruit on 20 December 1880, when, in a brief and fierce engagement, Commandant Frans Joubert routed Colonel Anstruther and 250 men and prevented reinforcements from reaching the small British garrisons stationed in several Transvaal towns. The key to the Transvaal, however, was Laing's Nek, on the border of Natal, where Commandant-General Piet Joubert and 800 men prevented Sir George Pomeroy Colley from entering the republic. On 28 January 1881 Colley's first assault was repulsed, and he decided to outflank the Boers by taking Amajuba, a flat-topped

peak of 2 000 m to the left of their position.

The Boers did not guard Amajuba at night, and on Saturday, 26 February, Colley began his assault with 554 men. On the way, he detached two groups, ordering them to entrench themselves, and occupied Amajuba at about 3 a.m. Joubert's wife, who had joined her husband at the front, was the first person to see the British, this being an unpleasant Sunday morning surprise for the Boer general. He gave his men a simple order: "You had better fetch them down." A party of 150 volunteers under Malan, Roos and Ferreira began to scale the crags under cover of diversionary fire. When they reached the top, the British fled in panic, and Colley, two officers and 82 men were killed, there being only one fatality on the Boer side.

This was a resounding victory which led to peace negotiations and the signing of the Pretoria Convention on 3 August 1881. The Transvaal gained self-government under the suzerainty of the British Crown, enough for the moment. On 16 December 1881 thousands of Boers gathered once again at Paardekraal to commemorate Blood River and give thanks for recent events.

The huge opencast diamond-mine at Kimberley is a hive of activity in this scene painted in 1876 by H. C. S. Wright. This mine, one of the biggest ever dug by man, can still be seen and is popularly known as "the Big Hole".

Treasures of the veld bring conflict

Towards the end of the 19th century the British colonies and Boer republics, relatively disparate, were being drawn together, not by political aspirations, but by a pursuit of economic power which not only generated conflicting territorial demands, but led to the fiercest and most protracted war ever fought on South African soil. This soil yielded two discoveries which were of great economic importance – first diamonds, and then gold.

In 1867, on the farm Kalk in the Hopetown district in the northern Cape Colony, a Boer youngster, Erasmus Stephanus Jacobs, picked up a sparkling stone in the veld and gave it to his sisters, who played games with stones. Later their mother showed the stone to a visitor, Schalk van Niekerk, who was sure that it was a diamond. Eventually the stone found its way to Dr W. G. Atherstone, in Grahamstown, who confirmed Van Niekerk's opinion, and rated the gem at 21,75 carats. The diamond was finally acquired by the governor of the Cape, Sir Philip Wodehouse, for £500. Shortly afterwards, a Coloured man brought Van Niekerk another stone, which he promptly obtained for 500 sheep, 11 heifers, a horse with its saddle and reins, and a gun. Van Niekerk sold the stone at Hopetown for £11 200, and, as the 83,5-carat Star of South Africa, it eventually fetched £25 000.

Diamond fever broke out, and everybody began looking for stones. Once finds had been reported with increasing regularity at the confluences of the Orange, Vaal and Harts rivers, thousands of fortune-seekers appeared. But the most important discoveries were made where Kimberley was to mushroom in a few years. Here diamondiferous soil was found in "pipes", and this changed the industry from a hunt along river beds to "dry" mining, and the largest opencast mine in the world. Soon diamond-digging was big business, and started to attract big businessmen.

Diamond-mining brought enormous personal wealth and power to Cecil John Rhodes, a young Englishman whose family had sent him to Natal in 1870, where his brother was farming, in the hope that the South African climate would heal a serious lung ailment. The two brothers soon left their struggling cotton plantation, and in Kimberley C. J. Rhodes became an exceptionally gifted businessman.

Cecil John Rhodes, diamond magnate, prime minister of the Cape Colony, and British imperialist.

A PARSON'S SON BECOMES THE KING OF DIAMONDS

Cecil John Rhodes was born the son of a parson in the English county of Hertfordshire on 5 July 1853. He was a bright but introverted and sickly boy who came to South Africa before he could enter a university. After making a fortune in Kimberley, he returned to study law at Oxford. By the time he had graduated he was barely 28, already very rich, and a member of the Cape parliament.

He was a product of the so-called "new imperialism", a major driving force throughout his life which made him dream of a "union of the English-speaking peoples throughout the world" which would include the United States. He had not the slightest doubt about the superiority of the British, declaring once: "I contend that we are the first race in the world, and that, the more of the world we inhabit, the better it is for the human race." Small wonder that his name became anathema to Afrikaners.

In 1881 Rhodes was elected to the Cape parliament as the member for Barkly West. In 1889 he founded, north of the Transvaal, the British South Africa Company – for commercial as much as for political reasons – and in 1890 he became prime minister of the Cape and one of the most powerful figures in South Africa. However, his increasing intervention in the affairs of the Transvaal in particular was to lead directly to one of the costliest and most destructive wars ever fought by Britain.

By 1880 he had formed the De Beers Mining Company, named after the family on whose farm an important find had been made. Another large undertaking was the Kimberley Central Company, controlled by Barney Barnato, a businessman who had come from London to the diamond-fields, while powerful French interests were also active. Competition began to depress the price of diamonds, but Rhodes proved himself master of the situation. In 1888 he merged his interests with Barnato's to form De Beers Consolidated Mines Limited. He began buying up the smaller companies, and ultimately controlled the diamond trade.

The rich diamond-bearing areas inevitably led to disputes about governmental jurisdiction. The Transvaal based its claim to the triangle between the confluence of the Vaal and the Harts River, north of it, on the Sand River Convention of 1852, and on agreements which Andries Pretorius had negotiated with the Black tribes in the area. The Orange Free State based its claims on the Bloemfontein Convention, which had given it independence north of the Orange River up to its confluence with the Vaal, and claimed some Transvaal territory as well, having bought it in 1861 from the Griqua chief Adam Kok. In addition, all the non-White inhabitants of the areas – which had once indisputably belonged to them – also lodged claims at the instigation of White agents. The first unsuccessful attempts to resolve the wrangles were made at Klipdrift in August 1870, at a meeting of all parties, and subsequently the British government became involved when the Griqua chief Nicolaas Waterboer appealed to the governor of the Cape for help. When the new governor, Sir Henry Barkly, arrived at the Cape in 1871 he had a ready-made pretext for annexing for Britain a most desirable piece of South African territory.

After avoiding an armed clash with forces sent by Barkly, President Brand, of the Orange Free

State, reluctantly agreed to accept arbitration by a British official, the lieutenant-governor of Natal, Robert Keate. In April 1871 all the aggrieved parties met in Bloemfontein. The Transvaal case was bungled by Pretorius, who was so sure of it that he omitted to submit important documents (while the opposition submitted falsified claims). On the submissions made to him, Keate had no choice but to reject the claims of the Orange Free State as well, and on 27 October 1871 the British annexed the disputed area. Brand disputed the decision tenaciously for five years, and finally settled for £90 000 in compensation – a paltry sum for what had been lost.

At least the economic stimulus of the diamond-

fields, and the compensation money, enabled Brand to develop and strengthen his republic. Irrigation projects were encouraged; roads, bridges and rail and telegraph links were established; and education was improved.

When Brand died in 1888, during his fifth term of office, he was succeeded by the chief justice, F. W. Reitz. Reitz consolidated his predecessor's work, signing a favourable customs treaty with the Cape, and making an important agreement with the Transvaal. Among other things, the two republics were to live in eternal peace with one another, and render mutual aid should a foreign power declare war. When, because of ill-health, Reitz retired in 1895, he was succeeded by Marthinus Theunis Steyn, the last leader of "the model republic". He worked ceaselessly for a great Afrikaner ideal: the unification of the Free State and the Transvaal and, ultimately, the whole of South Africa under a republican flag. During his term of office agriculture·achieved an unprecedented prosperity.

While diamonds were the chief preoccupation of the Orange Free State, the discovery of gold became the dominant factor in the Transvaal. The republic's first official gold inspector was appointed on 6 December 1853. He was Pieter Jacob Marais, who, like many after him, concentrated on alluvial gold. The first important discovery of gold-bearing ore occurred in the northern Transvaal, near Pietersburg, in October 1871, and, while various other strikes and the occurrence of alluvial gold were sporadically recorded, bringing in their wake the usual waves of adventurers and prospectors, the fabulous riches of the Witwatersrand had not yet been found.

From 1883 onwards, two brothers, Fred and Harry Struben, had been systematically exploring the area. Two years later, they employed a down-and-out prospector, George Walker, as a construction hand. Later, Walker was to claim that he had

Bloemfontein, capital of the Orange Free State Republic, in 1877. Although the diamond-fields went to Britain by arbitration, the Free State prospered in the years following the discovery of diamonds and became known as "the model republic".

Left: Some Black tribes of southern Africa "panned" alluvial gold by catching it in cattle-skins which were later dried. Gold-bearing sand was also washed by hand. *Right*: White prospectors, who had been prospecting since the 1850s, used contemporary panning methods.

discovered the main reef one Sunday morning in February 1886, on his way to visit a friend, George Harrison, who was also a prospector. Walker said that he stumbled over a piece of rock which he recognized as gold-ore. There is indisputable documentary evidence, however, that it was Harrison who lodged a prospector's claim in respect of the area; this Walker never did, and so it is Harrison who is generally regarded as the discoverer of the richest single gold-field in the world.

In June 1886 an experienced prospector, J. G. Bantjes, found an extension of the main reef (which, in turn, was successfully traced by the Struben brothers), and the Transvaal gold rush became a torrent. By the end of the year, with tent towns springing up like mushrooms, the site for the future city of Johannesburg – initially occupied by tin shanties – had been surveyed and officials had been appointed to maintain law and order.

As with diamonds, so with gold: trade and commerce flourished as never before, and vast new markets were created for the farmers' products. The State coffers of the Transvaal were filled to overflowing, and property prices rocketed, as every farmer was convinced that there was gold on his land. A wave of prosperity and wealth passed over a once poor and isolated Transvaal, and brought in its wake an era of extraordinarily rapid development, largely spearheaded by the railways.

The first railways

The first railway line in South Africa, only 3,2 km long, extended from the market-square, Durban, to the Point, Durban Bay. Trains covered the distance in five minutes, and were used primarily to transport goods from the harbour to the town. As this line was inaugurated on 26 June 1860, it is the first complete railway line in South Africa. But it was by no means the most important one, nor had Natal taken the lead in South Africa. As early as 10 October 1838 a railway at the Cape had been proposed in *The South African Commercial Advertiser*, and in 1853 the Cape Town Railway and Dock Company was established. It began building its first line, from Cape Town to Wellington, on 3 March 1859. Its first locomotive arrived on 8 September and was used to haul construction

materials as the line progressed – months before the Durban line was opened. The Cape line was inaugurated on 4 November 1863, the governor, Sir Philip Wodehouse, being one of the guests of honour. A line was also constructed from Cape Town to the southern parts of the Peninsula; it eventually reached the naval base at Simonstown in 1890.

The discovery of diamonds in the interior was the incentive behind the development of an extensive rail system. In 1873 the Cape Government Railway was formed, taking over the interests of smaller private companies. Two years later, 245 km of track had been opened in the Cape Colony, and ten years later the length had increased almost eight-fold. By the time the railway to the diamondfields had been completed in 1885, the colony boasted over 2 740 km of track. In the Transvaal, in 1875, President Burgers had already made an unsuccessful attempt to establish the republic's independence by building a rail link through Portuguese territory to Delagoa Bay. The paltry £93 833 he managed to raise in Holland for this purpose sufficed only to buy some material in Belgium. It was delivered at Delagoa Bay, where it rusted away as the project foundered.

But by 1887, with gold-mining operations in full swing on the Witwatersrand, the Transvaal government had more than enough revenue, and established the Nederlandsch-Zuid-Afrikaansche Spoorwegmaatschappij, which finally completed the rail link with Delagoa Bay in 1894. This had been preceded by the vigorous expansion of the Cape and Natal railways. The Cape railhead was within a few kilometres of the Transvaal border; the Natal line from Durban was nearing completion; and a second line through the Cape was approaching from Port Elizabeth. When it reached the Orange Free State, the Cape Government Railways offered to continue it to the goldfields, but President Kruger, of the Transvaal, was opposed to this. While he realized that he would not be able to prevent the British railways from reaching the Transvaal, he wanted his country's link with Delagoa Bay established first so that Transvaal would not be dependent on lines controlled by the British colonial government. But the Orange Free State gave way, and by 1890 the Cape link had been extended to Bloemfontein. This put Kruger under such pressure that, reluctantly, he had to agree to the continuation of the railway. The Cape link reached Johannesburg in 1892, and was joined a few months later by the railway from the eastern Cape. In 1895, when the railway from

From the time of its discovery in the Transvaal in the last quarter of the 19th century gold played a predominant role in South African history. Even today it is a major factor in South Africa's economy and relations with the rest of the world. Symbolizing the historical as well as the present importance of gold is the Kruger Rand, a coin consisting of one fine ounce of gold of 0,999 purity. On one side of the coin appears the head of Paul Kruger, president of the ZAR (Transvaal Republic) during the fateful last two decades of its existence. The design is the same as that used for gold coins of the ZAR in Kruger's time. A springbok appears on the reverse side. Kruger Rands have been coined since 1965 and are marketed in and outside South Africa, the price being determined by the free gold price.

The dawn of a new era is amusingly caught in this drawing by Heinrich Egersdörfer. A steam locomotive astonishes travellers still using an ox-wagon.

Durban had reached the Witwatersrand, all the most important centres of southern Africa were enjoying the benefits of an economic infrastructure that had developed with extraordinary rapidity.

The London Convention

Political developments in the Transvaal after its First War of Independence and the signing of the Pretoria Convention in August 1881 had become a tenacious struggle between British imperialism and fiercely independent Afrikaner nationalism in the republic. Before the war, Kruger had been to London twice to plead the Transvaal's case, and the largely successful outcome of the Pretoria Convention was due in no small measure to his statesmanship. The grateful republic made him its president and, on 9 May 1883, Stephanus Johannes Paulus Kruger was sworn in at Church Square, Pretoria. Once again, for the third time in seven years, he went to negotiate with the British, accompanied by General N. J. Smit and the recently appointed superintendent of education, the Rev S. J. du Toit. The new London Convention, signed on 27 February 1884 after nearly four months of negotiation, regained a series of important rights for the Transvaal. It was to be known once again as the Zuid-Afrikaansche Republiek and not the Transvaal State, as provided for in the Pretoria Convention, and there was no reference to British suzerainty. The agreement acknowledged the republic's independence and its right to its own Native policy, and restored to it a foreign policy subject only to British approval of treaties with foreign powers and with certain Black tribes. Britain no longer had the right to move troops through the Transvaal; the British Resident was to be replaced by a consul; the western border of the republic was extended; and the national debt was substantially reduced by £131 000. The deputation had every reason to be satisfied with its mission.

The New Imperialism

Far from relinquishing power through the London Convention, Britain had no intention of allowing the two Boer republics, with their rich mineral resources, to develop into powerful states which would threaten British supremacy in southern Africa. A new approach was adopted, a policy of encirclement. This meant surrounding the republics with British territory to prevent independent access to the outside world, and restricting them economically and in other ways so that they would be compelled to seek closer union with the British colonies. The results of this policy are exemplified by the development of the railway lines, and its causes can be found in the rising tide of "new imperialism". This, in turn, had two root causes: the worldwide rise of nationalism after the Napoleonic conquests, and fierce international competition for the commercial advantages to be gained from overseas possessions. Two fiercely opposed forces inexorably burgeoned in Southern Africa, and led to the collision between Rhodes, the British imperialist, and Kruger, the Afrikaner nationalist.

Afrikaner nationalism also revived at the Cape, where Rhodes reached the peak of his power when he became prime minister in 1890. Rhodes fully recognized that Afrikanerism was a force to be reckoned with, and relied heavily on the endeavours of the leader of the Afrikaner Bond, J. H. Hofmeyr, to establish a unified South Africa with equal rights for British and Dutch Afrikaners.

39

Rhodes also knew that the Afrikaner wanted his language recognized, as indicated by the Afrikaans language movement begun at Paarl, and thus, at the Bond's insistence, he re-introduced the use of Dutch in the law-courts and by the civil service. The Afrikaner Bond, which was ostensibly an agricultural organization, also obtained protective tariffs for Cape produce, while Rhodes saw to it that certain educational measures were instituted at the Bond's insistence. It is, therefore, understandable that he was supported by Hofmeyr and the Afrikaners at the Cape, and probably felt that he had neutralized local Afrikaner nationalism as a significant force. Events were to prove him utterly wrong.

In the Orange Free State, which had, by and large, maintained a cordial relationship with the Cape, there was, nonetheless, a bitter residue of resentment against Britain, because of the loss of the diamond-fields, and deep suspicion about any move by the British colony to extend its hold over the two Boer republics. In the Transvaal there was the same legacy, while the discovery of gold resulted in another problem which was to develop into a direct threat to Afrikaner supremacy on its own ground. The gold rush naturally attracted thousands upon thousands of foreigners to the gold-fields. These the republicans called *Uitlanders* ("Outlanders"). They were foreign not only in language, but in culture and religion, and threatened to overwhelm the indigenous White population by sheer force of numbers. Kruger was rightly concerned that the *Uitlanders* might one day take over the government, changing everything the Afrikaner had stood for for well over a century, and thrusting aside traditional national values.

At first, Kruger tried to give the *Uitlanders* a voice in the affairs of the Transvaal by instituting a

A TARIFFF WAR BECOMES A POLITICAL ISSUE

Once the Delagoa Bay railway had been completed in 1894, the Cape government railways were faced, inevitably, with a loss of traffic on lines which they had been operating very profitably and without competition for two years. They lowered their rates. Kruger retaliated by tripling the rates on that part of the Cape line which ran across Transvaal territory. To him it was important that preference should go to the Delagoa Bay line, and that he should show Rhodes that the Transvaal was not dependent on the Cape line.

In April 1895 a conference failed to break the deadlock, and so the Cape built a branch line to Viljoensdrift, a ford or *drift*, across the Vaal River which was a mere 60 km from Johannesburg. From Viljoensdrift, goods could be transported by ox-wagon.

In October 1895 Kruger took the drastic step of closing the *drift*, provoking an equally strong reaction from Rhodes, who saw in the situation a golden opportunity of bringing the Transvaal to heel. He interpreted Kruger's action as a violation of the London Convention and got the backing of Chamberlain, the British Secretary of State for the Colonies, for armed force, if necessary. An ultimatum from Chamberlain left Kruger no choice but to back down if he wanted to avoid war.

second *volksraad*. But it was thoroughly subservient to the original *volksraad*, and franchise qualifications were difficult to achieve. While many non-nationals preferred wealth to a vote, powerful British and foreign commercial interests wanted to foment discontent on the Rand so as to achieve their own political and economic ends. This agitation was so extensive among *Uitlanders* interested in political power that, in 1892, it gave rise to an organization called the Transvaal National Union. In 1895 the Union presented Kruger with a petition bearing 13 000 signatures, insisting on fairer enfranchisement; further petitions followed. Kruger felt quite unable to comply with the Union's demands, even though it is manifestly clear today that the franchise conditions were unduly onerous.

The Jameson Raid

Meanwhile, as early as 1894, Rhodes had begun to consider the exploitation of the *Uitlander* issue to bring down the Transvaal Republic. Despite encirclement, the Transvaal railway line had reached Delagoa Bay. Rhodes had been unable to get Kruger's support for a united South Africa under the British flag, a proposal thinly disguised as a South African customs union. This was rejected by Kruger. With the concurrence of Lord Roseberry, the British prime minister, Joseph Chamberlain, the Colonial Secretary, and Sir Hercules Robinson, the British high commissioner in South Africa, Rhodes set about organizing a *coup d'etat.*

It was to begin with a rising in Johannesburg supported by a military raid into the Transvaal by Dr Leander Starr Jameson, administrator of Mashonaland, on the northwestern border of the Transvaal. If this scheme succeeded, Robinson was to go to Johannesburg as a "mediator" between the Transvaal government and the National Union. As a result, a constituent assembly was to opt for self-government under British protection, and a federation of South African states.

Elaborate and detailed preparations were made by the so-called Reform Committee, but Rhodes miscalculated twice. According to his information, there were 100 000 British subjects in the Transvaal as against 14 000 Boers, whereas the actual figures were nearer 150 000 republican citizens, and only 41 000 British out of a total of about 76 000 *Uitlanders*. Neither was there any real enthusiasm for a rising, while there was dissension even among the conspirators. In addition, it is clear that Kruger and his government were fully aware of the plot. At the last moment, the leaders of the revolt in Johannesburg tried to call it off, but an impulsive Jameson and 500 hand-picked men of the Chartered Company (Rhodes's private police force) crossed the western border on the evening of 29 December 1895.

The Boer commandos, called up the following day, forced Jameson to surrender on 2 January 1896.

The abortive Jameson Raid, as it was known, was the downfall of Rhodes. In the Cape Colony he lost the support of the Afrikaner Bond; indeed, some members already distrusted him because he had threatened to use force after the closing of Viljoensdrift. Moreover, the Raid consolidated and intensified Bond support for Afrikaner nationalism. Rhodes resigned as prime minister, and also as managing director of the Chartered

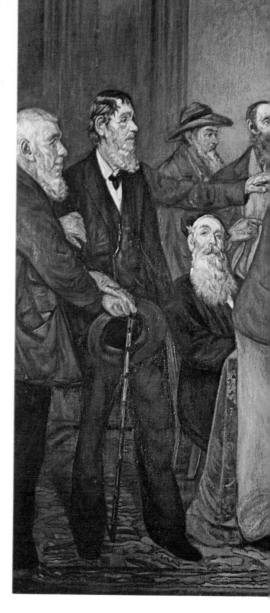

President Paul Kruger (seated, right) and his executive council receive a deputation of Transvaal citizens. After the discovery of gold the Transvaal Republic became an economic power frustrating the imperialism of Cecil John Rhodes. (Painting by F. Wichgraf.)

Company. Kruger magnanimously handed Jameson and his officers over to the British for punishment which was more or less perfunctory. In Johannesburg the Reform Committee attempted an insurrection which was doomed to failure. When the four leaders condemned to death on charges of high treason were given commuted sentences of a fine of £25 000 each, Rhodes paid the fines. For a time the *Uitlanders* were thoroughly subdued, but tension soon mounted between the British and the Afrikaner factions. The Transvaal began to arm itself, and in 1897 concluded a mutual-support alliance with the Orange Free State.

Last efforts to avoid war

British policy could follow only one course: interference in the domestic affairs of the republic because of the *Uitlander* franchise. This policy was adopted by Chamberlain and the new high

commissioner in South Africa, Sir Alfred Milner, both still under the impression that foreigners were in the majority in the Transvaal. When negotiating, it became increasingly clear to Kruger that Milner was uncompromisingly bent on war. At the beginning of 1899 Milner sent a petition with 21 684 signatures to Queen Victoria; in it her subjects on the Witwatersrand listed their grievances against the Transvaal government. The acceptance of the petition amounted to open confrontation with the Transvaal. The negotiations which followed at Bloemfontein were intended simply to gain time for Britain to move her forces as close to the Transvaal border as possible.

President Steyn, of the Orange Free State, had been making strenuous efforts to avoid war, and by September 1899 Kruger was prepared to grant to all *Uitlanders* a reasonable franchise qualification: five instead of fourteen years' residence. The British government, however, made further demands, and both leaders knew that the writing was on the wall. In obtaining his *volksraad's* support for the Transvaal, President Steyn said: "I would rather lose the independence of the Free State with honour than retain it with dishonour." Kruger sent the British a 48-hour ultimatum which expired at 5 p.m. on Wednesday, 11 October 1899. War had broken out.

A LEGENDARY FIGURE RISES FROM HUMBLE BEGINNINGS

The most widely known 19th-century Afrikaner statesman, "*Oom Paul*", as his people were later respectfully to call him, was born on 10 October 1825 to the descendants of *trekboers* in the Cape Colony. He had virtually no formal schooling, and is known to have been a sturdy, adventurous young boy.

Kruger's parents joined Potgieter's trek when it passed them in the southern Free State, and remained with it after the fateful Battle of Italeni, in which young Dirkie Uys and his father, Piet, lost their lives. In 1839 Kruger took part, for the first time, in a punitive expedition against the Ndebele, and in the same year – he was fourteen – he shot his first lion.

In 1842 he married – he was 17, and his bride, Maria du Plessis, was 16 – and began farming near the present town of Rustenburg, where he also hunted. He had, however, a highly developed love of his natural environment, and decades ahead of the time when game conservation became fashionable, he established the Sabie Nature Reserve, later the world-famous Kruger National Park.

Kruger's wife and their only child died in 1846, and the following year he married his wife's cousin, Gezina, by whom he had 16 children and who remained his faithful support until her death in 1901. He was assistant field-cornet of his area at 17, becoming a field-cornet eight years later, and thus attending with Pretorius the negotiations which led to the Sand River Convention. This was his first appearance in a public life.

While he was militarily active whenever necessary, Kruger's major concern was reconciliation between his individualistic compatriots – a never-ending task. In 1864 he was elected commandant-general of the Transvaal. He thus became a member of the executive council, but resigned from it in 1873 because he felt that he could no longer support President Burgers.

Before he could oppose Burgers in an election, Shepstone had annexed the Transvaal, and Kruger was sent on his first mission to London.

The Second Anglo-Boer War

About 80 years before the Anglo-Boer War broke out in October 1899, Lieutenant-Colonel John Graham imposed law and order on the eastern frontier of the Cape Colony with the help of large burgher commandos. His assessment was: "I never in my life saw more orderly, willing and obedient men than the Boers, and, whenever they have been engaged, (they) have behaved with much spirit, and always most ready and willing to go upon any enterprise." While the staff of the British War Office, who had been considering strategy against the two Boer republics from 1896 onwards, certainly did not underestimate the fighting abilities of the forces they were about to face, they could not have dreamt that the war would cost the British Treasury £191 million. Nor was Britain united about a conflict which the Liberal Opposition in parliament, under Sir Henry Campbell-Bannerman, fiercely condemned as an unjust war forced on the Boers by Rhodes, Chamberlain, Milner and Lord Salisbury.

President Kruger proclaimed martial law in the Transvaal, and in the Orange Free State President Steyn mobilized his burghers in accordance with the treaty between the two republics. Most of the commandos had been called out and had established themselves on the borders of Natal and the Cape Colony. They began moving to the five fronts which took shape at the beginning of the war. They were northern Natal; the border of Basutoland; the Orange Free State's western area, with Kimberley as its centre; the western area of the Transvaal, with Mafeking as its centre; and the northern area of Transvaal.

During the struggle, the Boer forces became a people's army. Boys as young as nine years old fought side by side with able-bodied men and grandfathers of over 70. About 52 000 men fought the war on the Boer side – 30 000 from the Transvaal, 20 000 from the Orange Free State, and 2 000 so-called Cape and Natal "rebels". At first, however, there were only about 35 000 armed Boers, numerically about equal to the British forces in the field at the time. Eventually, the British forces were, however, to outnumber the Boers four to one, and altogether 448 725 men saw service on the British side during the war.

The British were well-equipped and armed with powerful artillery; the Boers had, at the most, 70 field-pieces. Important arms ordered had not yet been received at the outbreak of the war, and eventually, as ammunition for their own Mausers ran out, the Boers had to rely almost entirely on the Lee-Metford rifles and ammunition they captured from the British. Ill-equipped, inexperienced in warfare, and hardly ready for action, the Boers had one considerable advantage: they knew the climate and terrain of their country; they were excellent riders and superb marksmen – an ideal, mobile guerrilla force fighting a disciplined but ponderous enemy.

French Creuzot cannon, known as "Long Toms", were used by the Boers at Mafeking and on the Natal front. Ponderous and difficult to handle, they were not entirely successful.

A Boer commando leaves a homestead. (An illustration based on a photograph taken on 17 February 1901 in the Orange Free State.)

Waiting for reinforcements, the initial British forces of about 27 000 soldiers (about half the total) were concentrated chiefly in northern Natal, and the rest were thinly spread over the key Cape railway links, apart from larger garrisons at Kimberley and Mafeking.

Like the British forces, the Boers were at first on the defensive. There is little indication that the Boer leaders realized the vital importance of decisive victories before a flood of reinforcements, or how easily they could have caused revolt in the Cape Colony if, at the outset, they had attacked there. Instead, the Transvaal commandant-general, Piet Joubert, and his 16 560 men, put pressure on the main British force in Natal. He achieved his first successes at Dundee and Modderspruit, forcing General Sir George White to retreat to Ladysmith, which was then besieged. Suddenly more than 80 per cent of the British forces were trapped.

At the same time, General Piet Cronjé and 5 000 men besieged Mafeking, wasting valuable time and men in a useless operation which was astutely prolonged for seven months by the British commander, Colonel Baden-Powell. Subsequently the same mistake was made at Kimberley (where, incidentally, Cecil Rhodes was trapped). Thus about 20 000 men were deployed in operations which were of no ultimate advantage to the Boers. Meanwhile, a few commandos on the Orange River had succeeded in declaring martial law in several nearby districts of the Cape Colony. This brought them widespread but numerically poor support from rebels in the colony.

A TELEGRAM THAT RAISED FALSE HOPES

After the Jameson Raid the German emperor, Wilhelm II, took an ill-considered step: he sent a telegram congratulating President Kruger on his success. This enraged the British, who saw it as interference in a domestic matter. They sent a naval force to Delagoa Bay to forestall any possible German support for Kruger. The telegram also inflamed public opinion in Britain; German sabre-rattling helped propagandists to camouflage the illegality of the Jameson Raid.

The telegram also raised false hopes in the Transvaal, for Wilhelm II soon realized that he was powerless against the British navy. When Kruger asked for the emperor's help after going into exile on 19 October 1900, he was refused an audience.

taken, principally Colesberg, Aliwal North and Burgersdorp. Methuen engaged the Boers on three separate occasions, first forcing the Free State commandant, Jacobus Prinsloo, to retreat, and then suffering severe losses when Prinsloo was reinforced by General J. H. de la Rey. Both withdrew to the Modder River, where they were joined by Cronjé, who had abandoned the siege of Mafeking. At the confluence of the Modder and Riet rivers, 3 000 Boers defeated the British forces on 28 November, until Cronjé withdrew unnecessarily to Magersfontein, while Methuen regrouped.

Then followed the second week of December 1899, the so-called "Black Week" of British armies, in which they were shatteringly defeated on the central, western and Tugela fronts. At Stormberg, after a gruelling night march, Gatacre, on French's right flank, was trapped near a railway junction. Free State men and Cape rebels under General J. H. Olivier attacked on 10 December and Gatacre's force suffered severe casualties. Two days later Methuen launched 12 000 men in a disastrous frontal attack on the Boer concentrations at Magersfontein, south of Kimberley. In a bloody battle the attack was repulsed by 8 000 burghers under De la Rey and Cronjé. The heaviest blow suffered by the British was, however, Buller's defeat on the Tugela on 15 December. Perturbed by the news of Stormberg and Magersfontein, Buller decided on a frontal attack on the positions of General Louis Botha, who had taken over from Joubert, who had fallen ill. Buller had to break through the Boer line to relieve Ladysmith, where White was still trapped. The engagement lasted nearly six hours, but Buller's massive infantry force of 23 000 men, supported by 42 guns, was beaten off by the superior marksmanship of 5 000 Boers. Buller had to retreat with 1 100 casualties and the loss of ten guns.

The jubilation in Europe and of the thousands of Boer sympathizers in Britain after the victories of "Black Week" was soon ended by the British War Office. Two divisions were already on their way to South Africa, and a third was almost ready to sail. Buller retained his Natal command, but was replaced as commander-in-chief by the 67-year-old veteran Field Marshal Lord Frederick Sleigh Roberts, V.C., the hero of Kabul and Kandahar, whose chief-of-staff was an equally distinguished soldier, Lord Kitchener of Khartoum. They arrived in Cape Town on 10 January 1900 and immediately began planning their main campaign.

Meanwhile, Buller made two more unsuccessful attacks on Botha's forces. With 30 000 men and 60 guns he attacked Botha at Spioenkop, but by 24 January he had been repulsed with 1 653 casualties. The Boers lost 50 men. Buller was repulsed for the last time at Vaalkrans, and abandoned the idea of reaching Ladysmith by crossing the Tugela River.

The tide turns against the Boers

The tide began to turn when Roberts started his offensive from the Cape Colony on 11 February 1900, exactly four months after the beginning of a war which was to last another two years and 109 days, as the Boer forces stubbornly and forlornly defended their freedom. Roberts had clearly defined objectives: with 30 000 men (four infantry divisions and a cavalry division under French) he wanted to relieve Kimberley, destroy Cronjé's main force, and occupy Bloemfontein. French adroitly bypassed Cronjé at Magersfontein and relieved Kimberley on 15 February, effectively proving the value of mounted troops which both sides were to use increasingly throughout the war (the British alone

Victories for the Boers

This was the situation towards the end of 1899, when General Sir Redvers Henry Buller, V. C., commander-in-chief of the British forces, disembarked at Cape Town with an army corps which brought the total British strength up to 50 000 men. This, it was hoped, would bring the war to a speedy conclusion. Buller regarded the Natal situation as so serious that he split his forces, instructing General Lord Methuen to advance on Kimberley with 9 000 men, while he went to Natal with the rest to relieve the hard-pressed British forces there. At this stage the Boers were fighting on British territory on all fronts. This situation lasted for almost four more months, but the Boers had lost an initiative which early decisive blows would have retained. When Buller arrived in Natal, the Boers were retreating north of the Tugela River to wait for his forces.

Three British groups were then advancing, two under Buller and Methuen, and one under General J. D. P. French, who, with Major-General Sir William Gatacre in support, was to drive the Boers from the Cape districts they had

THE FLOWER OF SCOTLAND IS CUT DOWN AT THE TRENCHES

The culmination of static trench warfare was in the First World War. But in the Anglo-Boer War trenches were often used as defensive firing positions and were easily abandoned. At Magersfontein, the brilliant tactician De la Rey had seen a further possibility: trenches could be used for an ambush.

Contrary to their usual tactics, the Boers did not occupy the hill at Magersfontein to secure a superior firing position. They took up a position lower down, reinforced by trenches in front of the foothills and commanding an extensive plain.

When Methuen's forces advanced early in the morning of 12 December 1899, under cover of darkness, the low, raking fire of the Boers took a devastating toll long before Methuen had expected an attack. Of almost 1 000 casualties, the heaviest losses were those of the Highland Brigade, the famous Black Watch. They also lost their commanding officer, Major-General A. J. (Andy) Wauchope, able, popular, and one of the most highly regarded Scotsmen of his time.

General J. H. de la Rey, one of the ablest of the Boer commanders in the Anglo-Boer War (1899-1902), won the Battle of Magersfontein.

used 350 000 mounts throughout the campaign). The Boers, tied up fruitlessly for so long at Kimberley, retreated to Boshof in the Orange Free State.

A turning-point in the war was the first great disaster to befall the Boers: the Battle of Paardeberg. Cronjé clung to his position at Magersfontein for too long before moving up the Modder River with a cumbrous column of ox-waggons and a large number of women and children who had joined the commandos. While General Christiaan de Wet and his Free State commando captured his first convoy of 176 waggons and 500 slaughter oxen from Roberts – who was bypassing the railway-line as a means of advance – the British pinned down Cronjé's forces at Vendutiedrift, east of Paardeberg, on 18 February. The encounter lasted ten days. The British were repeatedly beaten off or fiercely attacked from outside the encirclement by De Wet's men, who were making every effort to save Cronjé. Roberts had lost 1 442 men before Cronjé, despite many pleas made to him to stand firm while De Wet tried desperately to fight his way through to him, surrendered on Majuba Day, 27 February. This was a hard blow, for the largest single Boer force ever captured, 4 000 men, mostly from the Transvaal, surrendered. Before the end of the month Roberts had achieved two of his three primary objectives. Only Bloemfontein remained.

On the same day the Tugela front finally gave way to Buller, who attacked Louis Botha's force of 5 000 with 40 000 men supported by 72 pieces of artillery. Not even the most heroic defence could withstand such an onslaught. The road to Ladysmith and its famished inhabitants was open. Their morale shattered, the Boers retreated despite the entreaties of President Kruger. With the men who had not gone home Botha regrouped in the vicinity of the Biggarsberg.

The main theatre of the war then shifted to the Orange Free State. General Christiaan de Wet was made chief commandant and attempted to block Roberts's advance on Bloemfontein, where the two presidents, Steyn and Kruger, drafted a dramatic joint appeal calling on Britain and all other European governments to stop the bloodshed and to restore peace on a basis acceptable to both sides in the war. Before there could be any response, Roberts succeeded in surrounding De Wet at Poplar Grove. But this extraordinary general, who was to prove a thorn in the flesh of the British, escaped without the loss of a man, even though his force was greatly

A British mounted patrol in the veld, carrying Indian Army lances.

The artillery of the *Zuid-Afrikaansche Republiek* on the Tugela front, 1899. (Based on a photograph annotated by General Louis Botha.)

demoralized. The British occupied Bloemfontein without opposition on 13 March, the day after the curt rejection of the joint presidential appeal by the British prime minister, Lord Salisbury.

The Boer government was evacuated to Kroonstad, and De Wet allowed his burghers to disband on the understanding that, later, they would voluntarily return to their commandos. On 17 March a council of war, at which Kruger and Steyn were present, was held at Kroonstad. It was decided to continue the unequal struggle. But strategy was to change. Commandos were to operate as small, independent units and not as a people's army, hampered by supply-waggons. Exploiting their increased mobility, they were to, mainly, attack the British lines of communication. This was the kind of guerrilla warfare which De Wet had already exploited with success, and he continued to do so with quicksilver unpredictability. The British regarded him as almost supernatural, for he seemed to appear and disappear wherever he chose. In his brilliantly successful role as a guerrilla leader, De Wet attracted support for the commandos from wavering burghers. As the war progressed, however, more and more Afrikaners became so discouraged that they went over to the British, sowing the seeds of long-lasting bitterness between these "hands-uppers" and the "bitter-enders", those who held out until the end.

Roberts then planned a broad sweep northwards on a line from Kimberley

to Ladysmith, advancing on the Transvaal from the Orange Free State and Natal with forces totalling well over 100 000 men. On 28 March General Piet Joubert died in Pretoria and was succeeded as the Transvaal commandant-general by 38-year-old Louis Botha. To stem the advancing tide, Botha had at his disposal scarcely 12 000 men and 28 guns, and, when the British march on Pretoria began on 3 May, there was little else he could do but fight small harassing actions. With British columns crossing the Vaal River everywhere, Roberts formally annexed the Orange River Colony on 24 May. Later, his only setback on the Vaal was at Roodewal, where on 7 June De Wet disrupted the rail link for more than a week, seizing invaluable British supplies of equipment and ammunition, and instilling confidence into the disheartened Boers.

But the outcome was a foregone conclusion. Two days before Roberts rode into Johannesburg on 31 May 1900, Kruger and his government left Pretoria and established themselves at Machadodorp in the eastern Transvaal. Even Kruger wavered momentarily, and his faith in the Boer cause had to be restored by President Steyn and the good news of Roodewal. Control of the western Transvaal was delegated to General De la Rey. The State Attorney, Jan Christiaan Smuts, and the Transvaal government moved to Waterval Onder (where Kruger had been living for some time), and thence to Nelspruit, where it was decided that the president, whose age prevented him from accompanying the commandos, should go to Europe to seek support for the republics, while General Schalk W. Burger was to act as vice-president. Steyn and Kruger parted on the Portuguese border, and from then it was the Free State president who personified the spirit of Boer resistance until the end.

The mobile war

The Free State government moved to the north-eastern part of the territory which Roberts by then regarded as a British possession. Its members moved from town to town until President Steyn joined De Wet in the field, where resistance continued. Roberts regarded this resistance as rebellion against the new government. Then came an ominous decision. The British forces were to burn down farmhouses near railway lines which were being destroyed, this being an admission of Britain's inability to end the war by military means. This policy, the result of fruitless pursuit of the guerrillas, led to the burning of crops and the killing of cattle, a scorched-earth policy which made post-war reconstruction doubly difficult. Not only was the country denuded agriculturally; the population became hopelessly embittered.

Roberts's entry into an almost empty Pretoria at two o'clock on 5 June 1900 was something of an anticlimax. On 1 September 1900 he formally annexed the Transvaal as a British colony. Superficially, the war was over; it was merely a matter of clearing the country of armed bands of Boers. This was a serious error of judgment, for the mobile war took on even greater proportions. It was

THE WAR IN FIGURES

	Boer casualties	British casualties
Killed in action or died of wounds	3 990	7 091
Wounded	Not known	19 143
Died of other causes	1 081	Not known
Suffered from disease	Not known	71 243
Died in p-o-w camps	1 118	0
	6 189	97 477
Died in concentration camps: Men	1 676	
Women	4 177	
Children under 16	22 074	
	27 927	

A potential generation of Afrikaners had been wiped out. The Boers had lost a war, but untold suffering had forged a nation with an iron resolve.

planned by Boer governments in the field, and fought under the command of the chief republican officers, De Wet and Botha, and, in the northern Transvaal, Christiaan Beyers. Commando discipline became stricter; the weak-spirited were weeded out of the fighting ranks; all supplies, rifles and ammunition were to be captured from the enemy; and artillery was abandoned in favour of mobility. This was a problem without precedent for British military strategists.

De Wet's exploits were typical of this phase of the war. Early in August he had completely eluded 30 000 pursuers and returned to the Free State, embarking on a recruiting campaign among laggards and waverers. Many of them dug up their rifles, broke their oath of neutrality, and rejoined the commandos. Between 1 and 5 September De Wet invested Ladybrand, and, until October, harassed one British garrison after the other in the south, successfully attacking a British force at Frederikstad on 24 October. Another hunt for De Wet made him decide to invade the Cape Colony. Two of his officers, General J. B. M. Hertzog and General P. H. Kritzinger, reached the Atlantic coast at Lamberts Bay and the Willowmore district of the Cape respectively, while De Wet turned round and escaped once more, this time to Senekal.

At the end of November 1900 Kitchener succeeded Lord Roberts as commander-in-chief, and began applying systematic counter-measures against the mobile commandos. Simultaneously, he introduced lines of blockhouses connected by barbed-wire, and concerted sweeps by mounted columns, as well as his most controversial measure: the establishment of concentration camps for non-combatants, principally women and children. Boer prisoners-of-war were sent to camps outside South Africa, and their numbers grew steadily in the 14 camps established in Ceylon, Bermuda, St Helena, and the uplands of India. By the end of the war these camps housed 26 600 men.

Concentration camps, however, were a different matter. Initially these had been established to protect homeless women and children trekking in the veld, but, after the last pitched battle – fought at Dalmanutha (Bergendal) on 26 and 27 August 1900 between Botha and Roberts – the camps were used for the systematic removal of women and children from their farms to prevent them from aiding their men with food or information. As the population in the concentration camps grew – by October 1901 there were 118 000 Whites and 43 000 Blacks in about 40 camps – conditions deteriorated badly. The mortality rate among Whites was 344 per 1 000, and at one stage the child mortality rate in the Kroonstad camp was 878 per 1 000 a year. The main causes were inadequate medical and administrative services, unsatisfactory rations,

dishonest contractors and inefficient officials. When the truth became known, the concentration camps raised a storm of indignation in Britain and all over the Continent, and the Liberal Opposition in the British parliament roundly condemned them as "methods of barbarism". Even Lord Milner, who was now the administrator of the two annexed territories, conceded that the camps were a mistake in principle as well as in practice. Unavoidably, they were to add to the legacy of bitterness engendered by the war.

In the end, Kitchener's vastly superior numbers brought the war to a close. The Boers were still "fighting and fleeing" with some success. Surprisingly enough, almost the whole of the north-western Cape was controlled by 2 600 men under General Smuts and his generals, Maritz, Malan, Van Deventer and Lategan. "The Lion of the Western Transvaal", General De la Rey, was still undefeated, as was a fearless De Wet in the Free State. Once again, Kitchener conceived a plan which was to lead to bitterness: he formed a corps of National Scouts, Boers prepared to spy on their compatriots in order to bring the war to an end. Those who joined the British forces – and by May 1902 there were about 1 500 of them – saw this as the only sensible way out of an exhausting struggle which was being waged with no hope of success by a dwindling group of diehards. But they could hardly expect to be forgiven by those whom they betrayed.

Peace

British conditions for peace were first proposed to General Louis Botha by the British government on 7 March 1901 at Middelburg, Transvaal, but they were rejected. Early in 1902 Kitchener renewed his efforts and found that the Transvaal vice-president, Burger, was willing to negotiate. From 9 to 11 April, Steyn and Burger consulted each other at Klerksdorp, and at last peace seemed in sight. The two republics each chose thirty delegates from their forces in the field. They discussed the position in a tent at Vereeniging. After a debate which began on 15 May, a commission of five members – Botha, De la Rey, Smuts, De Wet and Hertzog – was appointed to negotiate with Kitchener and Milner in Pretoria according to the dictates of their consciences. Milner proved highly intractable and insisted, in opposition to Kitchener, on granting as little as possible. The agreement was taken to Vereeniging, where a three-day debate ended with a vote of 54 to 6 in favour of surrendering the independence of the republics. At 11 p.m. on 31 May 1902 the Treaty of Vereeniging was signed at Kitchener's headquarters in Melrose House, Pretoria.

A political map depicting South Africa at the end of the Anglo-Boer War (1899-1902).

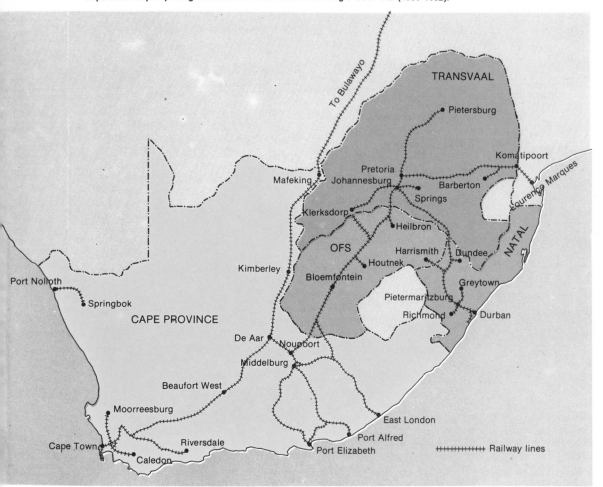

THE LAST YEARS OF A LONELY EXILE

Paul Kruger was in his 76th year when, on 19 October 1900, he left Lourenço Marques on the Dutch cruiser *De Gelderland*, which, provided by the young queen, Wilhelmina, brought him to Europe. He landed at Marseilles on 22 November, and wherever he went in France, Germany and the Netherlands he was received with great cordiality and respect. But no European government would openly support the Boer cause.

On 20 July 1901 Kruger's wife died in Pretoria, and the Peace of Vereeniging was signed on 31 May 1902 – heavy blows to an old man in ill-health. The British authorities were prepared to let Kruger settle in the Cape Colony (but not to return to the Transvaal), but he could not stomach the thought of once again becoming a British subject. Eventually the president and his party of a few relatives and officials occupied a house at Clarens, on the shores of Lake Geneva. There Paul Kruger died on 14 July 1904, shortly after sending a message to the Boer leaders, encouraging a defeated people to rebuild their future from the ashes of the war. "Who would create a future for himself," he wrote, "may not lose sight of the past. Therefore, seek in the past all that is good and noble that may be discovered therein, and shape your ideal accordingly." Kruger's remains were laid to rest in his former capital, Pretoria, on 16 December 1904.

The national convention was an extraordinary assembly of Afrikaans and English-speaking politicians. This scene, based on a photograph, depicts an informal moment during the final deliberations in Bloemfontein in 1909, with the Boer general Louis Botha and the arch-imperialist Leander Starr Jameson in conversation in the foreground.

British domination creates a new state

Vereeniging had established British supremacy in unequivocal terms. All White states in southern Africa were now subservient to the British Crown, but that supremacy still had to be consolidated. The war had not decided that South Africa would remain a permanent part of the British Empire; it had only made it possible. Lord Milner, a man of almost monkish dedication to the imperialist ideal, a man who described himself as a British race patriot, set about realizing that possibility with the considerable energy, intellect and power at his command. Shortly after the outbreak of the war he had begun formulating the steps he intended to follow, and, in December 1900, eighteen months before the war ended, he presented his programme in detail in a memorandum. The British population in South Africa was to be increased by immigration until it outnumbered the Afrikaners. A thoroughly Anglicized education policy was to be introduced, so as to push Dutch into the background as far as possible, even though clause 5 of the peace treaty had stipulated that Dutch could be taught in schools in the Transvaal and the Orange Free State, and, where necessary, would be used in courts of law. Only after these policies had established British rule would the former Boer republics be allowed to relinquish their status as colonies of the Crown.

Milner's first task was, however, to repair the ravages of war in the conquered territories. This was doubly difficult because of the scorched-earth policy introduced by Roberts and Kitchener. In this Milner was ably assisted by a group of young Oxford men whom he had gathered about him. Today they would be called "whizz-kids", but at the time they became known as "Milner's kindergarten". (Among them was John Buchan, who later wrote a famous adventure novel, *The Thirty-Nine Steps*, which included a character based on his experiences in South Africa.)

The problems of repatriation and resettlement in the two republics were enormous. About 31 000 Boer prisoners-of-war and 116 500 civilians in concentration camps (Milner put the figure at 155 000), as well as 100 000 Blacks in the camps, and about 50 000 *Uitlanders*, had to be resettled in areas where at least 30 000 homesteads, as well as crops and cattle, had been destroyed. New roads, railway lines and public buildings were also urgent necessities. By March 1903 repatriation had, on the whole efficiently, been completed, the cost being £16 500 000 to the British government in grants, non-interest-bearing loans and compensation.

Material reconstruction

South Africa's principal means of economic recovery was not, however, agriculture, but the exploitation of her gold-mines. Mining interests were finding it difficult to do this successfully, principally because of a shortage of unskilled labour, which, in November 1903, was estimated at 129 364 men. Once again, labour was imported from the East, this time from China. Altogether 62 200 Chinese labourers came to the Transvaal, and the value of gold production rose by 117 per cent to £27 401 000 between 1903 and 1907. The decision to use Chinese labour caused considerable political dissatisfaction, and was one of the factors which re-awakened political consciousness among the Boers, as well as further resentment against Milner and the British. Although the last of these indentured labourers left South Africa in 1910, there are still several small, culturally strong Chinese communities in the country.

By 1905 Milner's policy of material reconstruction was beginning to bear fruit. But he had little

The national convention in session. In the centre is the president, Sir Henry de Villiers, chief justice of the Cape. This painting by Edward Roworth hangs today in the dining-room of the Houses of Parliament in Cape Town.

SOUTH AFRICA SEES THE BIRTH OF *SATYAGRAHA*

Even before the Anglo-Boer War, Indians had migrated to the Transvaal, where a political colour bar was quickly instituted, but leniently applied. Contrary to Indian hopes, these laws were applied even more strictly by Milner and Selborne. The Indians' leader, Mohandas Karamchand Gandhi, was a British-educated barrister who had come to Durban from India in 1893.

In September 1906 Gandhi was successful in getting the Colonial Secretary to disallow a new registration ordinance for Indians, but one of the first acts of the new Transvaal parliament was to pass a law which introduced fingerprint registration. Gandhi organized a campaign of passive resistance based on the principle of non-violence (*satyagraha*), a method which was developed during the agitation for civil rights for Indians in the Transvaal, and which, 40 years later, was to have far-reaching consequences in India.

Gandhi's passive resistance resulted in numerous arrests, including his own, and, although he and Smuts reached a temporary understanding in January 1908, the matter was by no means settled. (In later years, Gandhi gave Smuts a pair of sandals which he himself had made, a gift which Smuts treasured to the end of his days.)

success in attracting British immigrants. His educational policy was also firmly opposed by the Dutch Reformed churches, which established schools based on the principle of "Christian national education". Meanwhile Afrikaans, as opposed to Dutch, was developing rapidly as a written language. It was nurtured by the works of a number of remarkable poets, another strong factor in the resurgence of the Afrikaner's national spirit. Nor did Milner provide any solution for South Africa's prevailing problem, "the Native question", as it was then called. On the whole, Milner was unsuccessful before he left South Africa in April 1905. He was succeeded by Lord Selborne.

Self-government

Selborne, whose initial policies differed little from Milner's, bore the brunt of the Afrikaner's resurgence. In January 1905 the first post-war Afrikaner party was formed in the Transvaal – *Het Volk* (The People), under the leadership of five Boer generals: Botha, Burger, De la Rey, Beyers and Smuts. Similar sentiments in the Orange River Colony (as the Orange Free State was then called) culminated in the formation of the Orangia Union in May 1906. It was led by Hertzog, De Wet (both generals in the Anglo-Boer War) and Abraham Fischer, a prominent politician in the Free State republic. These were all men who had remained faithful to the Boer cause. This gave them the backing of their compatriots and ensured that a party system would be functioning when there was any form of self-government.

On 12 January 1906, the Unionist (Conservative) government, which had been in power in Britain since 1895, was decisively defeated. The Liberal succession, under Sir Henry Campbell-Bannerman, was to prove significant for South Africa. He was the man who had vigorously supported the Boers when he was in opposition; this meant immediate rapport between the Boer leaders and the new British government. The Unionists had been considering limited self-government for the ex-republics, with an elected parliament, but a cabinet appointed by the British government. Smuts, who had gone to Britain even before Campbell-Bannerman's success, had considerably influenced his thinking. Campbell-Bannerman rejected the Unionist proposal and, in April 1906, appointed his own committee of investigation. This resulted in the promulgation of responsible government in the Transvaal in December 1906, and in the Orange River Colony in June 1907. Both were to have bicameral parliaments with their own cabinets.

Het Volk and the Orangia Union won the elections. In February 1907, Botha took office as prime minister of the Transvaal, Smuts becoming his right-hand man, and in November of that year Abraham Fischer became prime minister of the Orange River Colony, Hertzog being the dominating member of his cabinet. This was an extraordinary development. Only five years after the end of the war, the men who had fought Britain were the political leaders of the conquered territories. Smuts and Botha regarded this as remarkable generosity and were convinced that reconciliation between Boer and Briton was the right policy. But

Hertzog was less impressed. He regarded it as merely the fulfilment of Clause 7 of the Treaty of Vereeniging, which guaranteed "ultimate self-government, to be granted as soon as circumstances permitted".

Earlier efforts to unite the four South African territories, efforts which went back to the days of Sir George Grey, had all failed, mainly because not all the territories had been under British control. Later, with all four areas enjoying more or less equal status determined by British control, closer association was a logical step for a number of reasons. One of them was that White South Africans of all political persuasions were agreed that "the Native question" could only be settled if there was a uniform policy everywhere. In Natal and the Cape the Blacks had the vote, but because of the franchise qualifications this was largely theoretical; they did not qualify for the vote in the Transvaal and the Orange Free State.

The problem was brought to the fore by the Bambata Rebellion in Natal in 1906. This was the culmination of widespread Zulu discontent with Natal's attitude to Blacks. While the Coloureds were obviously entitled to the vote in the Cape, there was some difference of opinion as to whether the Treaty of Vereeniging excluded them from enfranchisement in the Transvaal. In addition, there was discontent among the Indians in Natal and the Transvaal. They were ably led by a young Indian barrister, M. K. Gandhi.

The national convention

Other problems affecting the common welfare of the four territories were unsound competition in trade and commerce, customs tariffs, and railway policy. Meanwhile, hostility between Britain and Germany was growing, and it was thought that a unified South Africa would mean inestimable advantages for the British Empire in a war with Germany. Clearly, circumstances were favourable for a union which was being considered more and more seriously by all South African statesmen. In January 1907 a document prepared by Lord Selborne and the few remaining members of "the Milner kindergarten" was circulated to the governments of all the South African territories and to Southern Rhodesia. It pointed out the advantages of unification for all White South Africans. At various conferences held in May 1908 at Pretoria and Cape Town, the idea gained support, and resulted in a national convention to consider a constitution.

The convention first met in Durban on 12 October 1908. It resumed its discussions at Cape Town on 23 November, and its final session at Bloemfontein began on 3 May 1909. It was a remarkable assembly of Afrikaans and English-speaking politicians under the presidency of Sir Henry de Villiers, chief justice of the Cape, Steyn, the former president of the Orange Free State, being the vice-president. Among the 30 delegates representing both the governing and opposition parties of the colonies were all four prime ministers: Botha (Transvaal), Fischer (Orange River Colony), John X. Merriman (Cape) and F. R. Moor (Natal); there was also a three-man observers' delegation from Southern Rhodesia. Among the other members were four more Boer generals (Smuts, De la Rey, De Wet and Hertzog), Jameson, whose unsuccessful raid had brought the Anglo-Boer War a step closer, and Sir Percy FitzPatrick, one of the *Uitlander* conspirators in the Transvaal and later the author of a South African classic, *Jock of the Bushveld*.

There were many problems to be solved, although the convention would never have been constituted if there had been no basic agreement about its purpose. One of these problems was the position of Natal, the only territory which, except for the few short-lived years of the first Voortrekker Republic, Natalia, had been constantly under British rule since its inception. As it feared domination by the Afrikaners, Natal distrusted a union with a centralized government and little regional autonomy. Its delegates preferred a federation, but realized that Natal would have to join whatever closer association would be proposed. Natal's fears were partially allayed by the provision made for a provincial council for each territory, a council which would have limited control over local services.

THE WORLD AT LARGE

1903 A treaty between the United States and Panama hands over the canal zone to American control.
1904 War breaks out between Japan and Russia.
1905 Workers in St Petersburg form the first soviet; mutiny on the battleship *Potemkin*.
1907 The giant steamers *Lusitania* and *Mauritania* are launched.
1908 King Carlos I of Portugal assassinated.
1909 Robert Peary reaches the North Pole.
1910 George V accedes to the British throne on the death of Edward VII.

Once again "the Native question", in the form of enfranchisement, was discussed. Some delegates supported the Cape system (universal suffrage for all citizens of the proposed union, subject to the customary qualifications), while others were totally opposed to any form of Black franchise. In the end, chiefly at the urging of Smuts, who could not bear to see the ideal of union founder on this issue, the convention took a decision which, in practice, simply shelved the problem: each area was to retain its current system. It was decided that there would be a bicameral parliament and that the British monarch would be represented in South Africa by a governor-general appointed by the British government.

Choosing a capital

There were other formidable obstacles, but the one which almost caused a deadlock was the choice of a suitable capital. The Cape delegates considered Cape Town, "the Mother City", the only logical choice. The Transvaal maintained that Pretoria was more central (geographically and economically), especially if Southern Rhodesia were to join a union – an option this territory rejected in a subsequent referendum. Natal supported the Transvaal, while the Orange River Colony hoped for a compromise: Bloemfontein, which geographically was central. The matter was settled by a decision worthy of Solomon: Cape Town was to be the legislative, Pretoria the administrative, and Bloemfontein the judicial capital (accommodating the Appellate Division of the Supreme Court of South Africa).

The draft of the South Africa Act, the proposed constitution for the Union of South Africa, was signed by all the delegates on 11 May 1909, and was overwhelmingly supported by the Whites when it was referred back to each parliament. In Natal a referendum also supported the South Africa Act by a large majority. Politically-conscious Blacks, however, objected strongly to the provisions which concerned them, and emphasized that they had not been given a hearing at the national convention. Black and Coloured conventions and protest meetings were held, and it was decided to ask the British government to change the franchise provisions of the Act that affected non-Whites. Led by W. P. Schreiner, a former prime minister of the Cape Colony, a delegation went to London. But, although the colour-bar restrictions were criticized in the British parliament and the prime minister, Herbert Asquith, appealed to South African statesmen to modify the franchise provisions, no amendments were made. The South Africa Act was signed by King Edward VII on 20 September 1909, and came into force on 31 May 1910.

This was exactly eight years from the day on which the Boers had capitulated by signing the Treaty of Vereeniging. The achievement was a remarkable one, considering the stormy history of the area and the wide differences of background and outlook separating the various participants in the convention. But, as Steyn pointed out, the millennium had not yet arrived. The first Union government was faced with wide-ranging and complex problems, and conciliation and compromise were unlikely in view of the fact that the most pressing problem, "the Native question", had remained unsolved. Three of the founders of the Union, all former Boer generals, were to dominate South African politics for almost 40 years. They were Louis Botha, the first prime minister; James Barry Munnik Hertzog, prime minister for fourteen uninterrupted years; and Jan Christiaan Smuts, twice prime minister, and an active politician until his death in 1950.

The first cabinet of the Union of South Africa was appointed before an election was held. Asked to form a cabinet by the first governor-general, Lord Gladstone, General Louis Botha chose his ministers from the governing parties of all the four former colonies. Standing at the back are from the left: Gen J. B. M. Hertzog, H. Burton, F. R. Moor, Dr D. G. O'Grady Gubbins, Gen J. C. Smuts, H. C. Hull, F. S. Malan and Sir David Graaff. Seated are J. W. Sauer, Gen Botha and A. Fischer.

Fifty years of Union

The first task of Botha's cabinet was to create a parliament by arranging an election date: 15 September 1910. The brevity of the pre-election period did not permit the formation of well-organized, national political parties, and the election produced the following results on the basis of loosely-knit common interests: the South African National Party in Transvaal (previously *Het Volk*) under Botha, the Orangia Union in the Orange Free State under Hertzog, and the South African Party and the Afrikanerbond in the Cape won 67 of the 121 parliamentary seats. The strongest Opposition group, the Unionists, under the leadership of Jameson, won 39 seats. This party was an amalgamation of the Unionists of the Cape, the Progressive Party of the Transvaal, and the Constitutional Party of the Orange Free State. The Labour Party, under Colonel F. H. P. Creswell, won four seats, while there were 11 independents, mainly from Natal, where reservations about the concept of union were still very strong.

Consisting of the groups supporting Botha, the South African Party (SAP) was formed in November 1911. But, fundamentally, divisions within the party were more serious than its differences with an Opposition which essentially was more closely linked to Britain, and more capitalistically inclined. In the SAP, Botha and his ablest supporter, General Jan Christiaan Smuts, represented a policy of reconciliation and "forgive and forget" between Afrikaans- and English-speaking people, the Boer ideal of an independent republic disappearing into the background while closer links with Britain were being forged. There were gestures such as the presentation to King Edward VII, in 1907, of the Transvaal's Cullinan diamond (the biggest ever discovered); Botha agreed to unveil the Rhodes Memorial on the northern slope of Table Mountain in 1912; he praised his English-speaking supporters. Such developments convinced many Afrikaners that

Botha was prepared to sacrifice too many of their interests to attract the support of English-speaking South Africans.

Hertzog, on the other hand, represented the undying republicanism of people like De Wet, De la Rey and Steyn (who would almost certainly have become the first prime minister of the Union had his health not been so bad). In contrast to Botha's "one-stream policy", advocating the merging of the two White language groups, "Hertzogism", as it was called, was regarded as the representation of oppressed Afrikaner nationalism. It recommended a "two-stream policy": the two White cultural heritages, it was maintained, should exist separately on the basis of absolute equality, perhaps meeting in a distant future; the relationship of the Union with Britain was not to be based on blind loyalty, but on practical expedience.

"South Africa first!"

An early rupture was thus inevitable. It was precipitated by a speech made by Hertzog at De Wildt, near Pretoria, on 7 December 1912. He made his slogan "South Africa first!", and said: "Imperialism meets my approval only in so far as it serves South Africa."

Botha's English-speaking supporters protested and one of his ministers tendered his resignation immediately. When Hertzog refused to resign from Botha's cabinet, Botha himself resigned. This meant that a new cabinet had to be formed. As he was the leader of the largest party, this was Botha's task, and Hertzog was discarded. At a congress at Bloemfontein in January 1914 Hertzog and his supporters decided to form the National Party. The long political struggle between "Nat" and "Sap" had begun.

Already uneasy relations became more strained when the First World War began on 4 August 1914. As a British dominion, the Union was unable to choose its own policy. It automatically participated as part of the British Empire. Naturally, the English-speaking population accepted this as a moral obligation. But that was not how Hertzog saw the matter. He wanted South Africa to remain neutral until it attacked.

"The age of the generals" began, among South African prime ministers, with Louis Botha (left) and Jan Smuts.

RULE BY BROAD CONSENSUS

Broadly speaking, the period from 1910 to 1943 was dominated politically by the thinking of Botha and, particularly, Smuts, whose South African Party (later the United Party) won most of the elections. Among its aims was a broadly based South Africanism, leaning towards Britain as a kind of "mother country". Even when the National Party, under Hertzog, dominated the 1924 and 1929 elections, it did so with the support of the predominantly English-speaking Labour Party, this leading to a coalition cabinet with Afrikaans- and English-speaking members.

When Hertzog and Smuts joined forces in 1934 to form the United Party, Malan and his small group decided not to join and remained a drastically reduced National Party.

The following table indicates the seats won by the parties at each general election, but does not take into account the complexities of by-elections, redelimitations, party mergers, special representatives and increases in parliamentary seats. Parties totally unsuccessful in the elections do not appear.

	1910	1915	1920	1921	1924	1929	1933	1938	1943
South African/ United Party	67	54	41	79	53	61	61	111	89
Unionists	39	40	25						
Labour Party	4	4	21	9	18	8	2	3	9
Independents	11	6	3	1	1	1	10	1	2
National Party		26	44	45	63	78	75	27	43
Natal Home Rule							2		
Dominion Party								8	7

Truly tragic consequences were to develop, however, from the misguided attempt by a third group of Afrikaners to restore an independent republic by force of arms. On 10 August Botha had already responded to a request from Britain that the Union should occupy South-West Africa, a German colony. When this became public knowledge in a heated debate in parliament in September, the plot to rebel gained considerable momentum. De la Rey and De Wet were involved, as were a number of high-ranking army officers, including the commanding officer of the recently established Union Defence Force, General C. F. Beyers, who resigned when he heard of Botha's plans.

De la Rey, who had turned against Botha only after much uncertainty, was the first to die unnecessarily. On 15 September, on his way to the military camp at Potchefstroom, he ordered his driver to ignore a police command to stop at a check-point. An order that they were not to shoot failed to reach the check-point in time, and De la Rey was killed by a single ricochet.

Plans for protest by the other leaders were vague, and none of them had sufficient influence to represent or organize the discontent of many Afrikaners. Matters came to a head, however, when a hot-head, Lieutenant-Colonel Manie Maritz, commander of a military camp at Upington in the north-western Cape, joined the Germans on 10 October and threatened to invade the Cape. Botha had to take what has been called the most difficult decision of his public life. On 12 October he declared martial law so as to control a situation in which Afrikaners were firing at one another. (It had been decided that only Afrikaans-speaking soldiers would be used to put down the rebellion.)

Shortly afterwards, malcontents in the Orange Free State and the Transvaal began forming commandos, and soon there were about 12 000 men under arms. Badly armed and unco-ordinated, none of the commandos was a match for government troops who forced one of the last groups under Captain Jopie Fourie to surrender near Pretoria on 16 December. Fourie had not resigned his commission before joining the rebels, and was court-martialled on a charge of treason. He was found guilty and sentenced to death. Smuts could have commuted the sentence, but deliberately avoided being forced to take action. He subsequently admitted that this was the greatest mistake of his political career, for Fourie's death became a lasting focal point for bitterness. Another death was that of Beyers, who drowned in the Vaal River while escaping from government troops. The last rebels, under Kemp and Maritz, surrendered on 2 February 1915; all were leniently treated.

Heroism on the Somme

South Africa's contribution to the global war was considerable. With Botha himself in command, the German forces in South-West Africa were overwhelmed by superior numbers and had to surrender on 9 July 1915. About 19 000 South Africans fought with the British forces in Tanganyika, where Smuts was given the command in February 1916. (Later he was succeeded by General Van Deventer.) But their wily German opponent, General Paul von Lettow-Vorbeck, survived until the end of the war.

The first South African volunteers left for the Western Front in November 1915, and soon distinguished themselves at Delville Wood, a key position on the Somme which they held in the face of an unremitting six-day enemy onslaught from 14 to 19 July 1916. But the losses sustained were dreadful: of 121 officers and 3 032 men, only five officers and 750 men escaped unscathed. During the war about 146 000 Whites, as well as nurses, Coloured troops, and 80 000 non-combatant Blacks, were in uniform; 6 006 lives were lost.

This record gained international recognition for South Africa, and Botha and Smuts in particular. Smuts had been a member of the British war cabinet. He virtually "fathered" the Royal Air Force; he played a prominent part in creating the League of Nations; and he correctly foresaw the dire consequences of "crushing" Germany through the Treaty of Versailles. But in South Africa the two war leaders lost ground to Hertzog. As early as 1915 the Nationalists had gained 20 seats in an election.

Botha died unexpectedly in August 1919 and was succeeded by Smuts, who lost even more ground in the next general election, held in March 1920. Efforts to reunite the South African Party and the National Party proved fruitless, as Hertzog insisted on the right to secede from the British Empire.

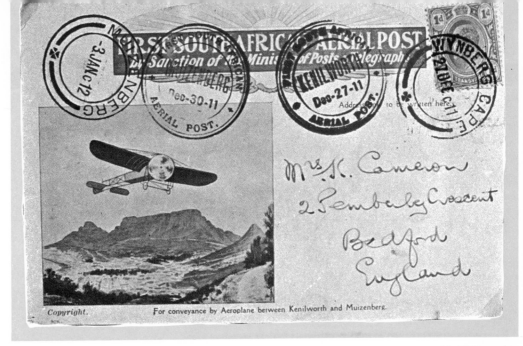

South Africa's first airmail service, between Muizenberg and Kenilworth, is commemorated by this cover dated 30 December 1911.

Smuts had to seek common ground with the Unionists. In February 1921 the strengthened SAP won 79 seats and the Nationalists 45. There were nine Labour Party members and one Independent.

In 1922 the government faced its most serious crisis since the rebellion. The industrial development of the country, and of the mines in particular, had created a class hitherto unknown – the skilled White worker, who was soon organized into trade unions. The first confrontation with the government came in the middle of 1913, when a trivial dispute about working conditions developed into a struggle with mine-owners for the recognition of the unions. Strikes and riots followed, and these Smuts and Botha could end only by meeting the demands of the miners: reinstatement of dismissed workers and a promise to investigate grievances.

The miners saw this as a victory and in January of the following year another strike broke out, at once assuming far larger proportions than the first. This time it was effectively quelled by the re-organized South African Defence Force, and Smuts autocratically deported nine of the ringleaders.

The depression which began in 1920 sparked off a third major strike in 1922, when the mine-owners proposed wage-cuts and a proportionately higher employment of Blacks. By 5 February the strike had become a large-scale revolt and by the end of the month several strikers died in a clash with the police. By 10 March Smuts could not avoid declaring martial law, and army detachments,

supported by Air Force units, crushed the strike four days later. At least 150 lives were lost. So was a great deal of support for the government, which was considered incapable of supporting White workers faced with the mine-owners, on the one hand, and the competition of Black labour, on the other.

When the next election was held in June 1924, Smuts lost to a united Opposition. The National Party and the Labour Party made an election pact not to oppose each other and won 83 seats (65 and 18 respectively) against the SAP's 53, and that of one independent. Hertzog was asked to form a government and gave two – later three – of the portfolios in his cabinet to Labour.

Hertzog becomes prime minister

Although Smuts called it an "unholy alliance" which would not last, the Pact Cabinet, as it became known, co-operated extraordinarily well and a great deal of constructive legislation was passed. A powerful steel industry was created through the establishment of the South African Iron and Steel Industrial Corporation (ISCOR), and important labour legislation was passed. Hertzog's personal triumph came at the imperial conference in London in 1926, where he pressed for the autonomy referred to in the Balfour Declaration, which made it clear that Britain and the Dominions were "equal in status, in no way subordinate to one another". Smuts assumed a rather lofty attitude and would not support Hertzog. He maintained that South Africa was perfectly independent, and pointed out that it had signed the Treaty of Versailles in its own right as a participant in the war.

Legal anomalies regarding the status of the Union were finally removed in 1931 with the adoption of the Statute of Westminster. It was only natural that South African and Afrikaner independence developed under Hertzog. In 1925 the conferment of British honours on South African citizens was abolished and on 8 May of the same year Afrikaans became the country's other official language, replacing Dutch. In 1928 South Africa's national flag was hoisted for the first time. But large-scale differences of opinion about the design account for the compromise it still is today.

Hertzog's National Party won the 1929 election

with an overall majority, but he retained two Labour members in his cabinet in appreciation of their previous support. Then a world-wide depression began to make itself felt in South Africa. Britain left the gold standard in 1931; this meant that it would no longer exchange South African Reserve Bank notes for the gold they represented. International uncertainty about currency resulted; the British pound became vulnerable to speculation, particularly as South Africa remained on the gold standard until the end of 1932. Fuelling the growing economic depression in South Africa was a lengthy drought which had ruined many farmers by the end of the same year. On top of unheard-of economic problems, Hertzog was confronted by a popular political maverick, Judge Tielman Roos, previously one of his leading supporters, who made a strong bid for the prime ministership.

On 15 February 1933 Hertzog reached a coalition agreement with Smuts and formed "a government of national unity" to combat the crisis, handsomely winning a snap election. But Dr D. F. Malan, Hertzog's minister of the interior, distrusted these developments, which he felt were detrimental to Afrikaner interests. When Hertzog and Smuts formally merged their parties in the United Party on 5 December 1934, Malan, who had not joined the coalition cabinet, broke away with 19 parliamentary followers and formed "the purified National Party".

Conflicting ideals

The coalition achieved some progress towards economic recovery, and introduced important measures affecting the Blacks. One act provided a basis for increasing the existing territories of the Blacks, and another removed Black voters from the common voters' roll in the Cape Province. Registered Black voters in the Cape were placed on a separate voters' roll and could vote only for three White representatives in the house of assembly, and two in the Cape provincial council.

Although the United Party won the election in 1938 with ease, continual tension resulted from the different ideals of Smuts and Hertzog, tension which came to a head with the outbreak of the Second World War. Hertzog wanted South Africa to remain neutral; Smuts considered that it was the country's "honour and duty" to support Britain. At a special session of parliament on 4 September 1939 Hertzog's neutrality motion was defeated by

General Louis Botha in conversation with the mayor of Windhoek after that city's peaceful capitulation to South African forces in May 1915.

80 votes to 67. Smuts took over the premiership and declared war on Germany two days later.

The break with Hertzog was the inevitable result of the simmering dissension in the United Party. Pro-British Smuts supporters had resented Hertzog's introduction of *Die Stem van Suid-Afrika* (*The Voice of South Africa*) as the official anthem of the country in 1938, and of the national flag in 1939. Both the British anthem and flag were retained for ceremonial occasions, but Hertzog's innovations were an erosion of symbols representing past British supremacy in South Africa which Smuts's supporters found hard to stomach.

Early in 1940, Hertzog and his followers took the logical step of joining Malan in a re-unified National Party under Hertzog's leadership.

South Africa in the Second World War

At the outbreak of war, South Africa had an army of 17 038 men, an air force of 1 837, and a navy of 432. Numbers increased rapidly, and at the cessation of hostilities 132 194 had served in the army, 44 569 in the air force, and 9 455 in the navy –

a total increase in the Defence Force of 865 per cent. To this should be added the contributions of 24 975 women and 123 131 non-Whites. South African soldiers fighting in foreign theatres of war gave their services voluntarily, and were engaged in four principal areas – East and North Africa, Madagascar and Italy. Many South African nationals joined other Allied forces, chiefly those of the British. For example, the South African fighter pilot "Sailor" Malan became a legend at Biggin Hill during the Battle of Britain, in which 13 South Africans died.

In North Africa the German General Rommel confronted Britain's Eighth Army. Two South African divisions fought throughout the desert war as part of the Allied forces, and the South Africans played a significant part in the climactic Battle of El Alamein, which began General Montgomery's successful offensive against the Axis forces. From 1943 onwards, the South African Air Force and the Sixth South African Armoured Division served in Italy as a part of the British Eighth Army and the American Fifth Army.

In the jungles and swamps of East Africa thousands of South Africans participated in a lengthy campaign against German guerrilla forces under General Von Lettow-Vorbeck.

Smuts in command

During the war Smuts retained his commanding majority in the election of 1943, and reached the pinnacle of his prestige. In 1941 he was made a field marshal of the British army. Subsequently, he played a major role in the establishment of the United Nations Organization, and wrote the preamble of the UNO charter. In his own country, however, his Afrikaner compatriots regarded him as a man who put Britain before South Africa. He had helped to win a global war, but was about to lose his last election.

Superficially the Nationalist Opposition still looked hopelessly divided; there had been serious disunity during the war. The *Ossewa-Brandwag*, for example, which in 1939 had begun as a cultural organization dedicated to Afrikaner ideals, had become paramilitary by 1941. One of its offshoots, the *Stormjaers*, went so far as sabotage in the hope of overthrowing the government and declaring an Afrikaner republic. These groups were suppressed by Smuts, but they were also rejected politically by the National Party, whose leaders deprecated all forms of unconstitutional or violent action.

Despite the "re-unification" of the National Party, there were serious differences between Hertzog and Malan, the most important issue being republicanism, which Hertzog did not regard as a goal for the foreseeable future. Hertzog's draft constitution for the party was rejected by a congress at the end of 1940. He regarded this as a vote of no confidence in his leadership and retired from public life. Two years later he died, and some of his hardline followers under N. C. Havenga – his minister of finance for 15 years – established the Afrikaner Party. Others, under Oswald Pirow, formed the New Order Party.

"Join together those who belong together!"

Malan's watchword was "Join together those who belong together!" This he always tried to do. By 1947 he had secured an election agreement with the Afrikaner Party that was vindicated in the election held on 26 May 1948. The coalition won by an overall majority of five seats, and even Smuts lost his seat at Standerton. (In 1951 the two parties merged to form the present National Party, which has governed South Africa ever since.)

Despite irritating shortages of imported commodities and food, the war had brought South Africa economic prosperity and a rapid development of industrialization which, in turn, led to an influx of Black labour to the cities. On the whole, the Smuts government had followed a *laissez-faire* policy, disconcerting to many Whites, and unsatisfactory to all races in South Africa. Internationally the post-war period had brought about the rejection of any form of racial discrimination because of what had been an odious feature of the Hitler regime in Germany.

At the UN foreign criticism of South Africa's traditional race policy was heard as early as 1946. Smuts had not succeeded in obtaining approval for the incorporation of South-West Africa into the Union, which had administered the territory as a mandate since the end of the First World War. But such criticism had only a negative effect. Whites in South Africa regarded the rise of the Blacks and the elimination of the colour bar as a threat to their survival, and had no intention of bowing to foreign pressures seeking change. Thus, when the National Party came to power in 1948, race relations became the most important aspect of the political future of South Africa.

In retrospect, 1948 was the year in which a decisive choice was made between two possible solutions of the colour question. Confronted essentially with integration or segregation, the electorate chose the latter, known as "apartheid" or "separateness", the first a term which was to attract worldwide notoriety. During the first few years of its term of office, the new government legislated for social segregation between White and Black. Separate facilities were to be provided for the different race-groups, intermarriage was prohibited, separate residential areas were demarcated, population registration on a racial basis was made compulsory, and there were efforts to resettle the urban Blacks in their traditional tribal areas.

After a lengthy constitutional fight, lasting from 1951 to 1956, the Coloured people in the Cape Province were placed on a separate voters' roll, as the Blacks had been in 1936, and given representation in parliament through four Whites. These and other laws of the time enforced apartheid, but did not affect the core of the race situation because they were not the answer to the problem of political rights for non-Whites, the largest part of South Africa's population.

After increasing the parliamentary representation of the National Party from 70 seats in 1948 to 94 in the elections held in 1953, Malan resigned as prime minister on 30 November 1954 at the age of 80. As his successor, the party caucus chose J. G. Strijdom, a determined Afrikaner who at one stage had been the only representative of the National Party in the Transvaal. Under Strijdom's leader-

ship the party once again increased its parliamentary strength in the general election of 1958, winning 103 seats – almost two-thirds of the parliamentary representation, while the United Party seats declined to 53, and the Labour Party disappeared. There were also three White representatives of Black, and four White representatives of Coloured voters.

Verwoerd: transforming apartheid into separate development

Strijdom died suddenly on 24 August 1958, and Dr H. F. Verwoerd became his successor. He, more than anyone else, was the architect of and the driving-force behind the policy of apartheid, and was chiefly responsible for transforming it from merely negative domination into a positive policy of separate development which aimed at "fairness to each and justice for all".

Hendrik Frensch Verwoerd, admired by supporter and opponent alike for his intellect, dedication and strong will, was born of Dutch parents on 8 September 1901, and came to South Africa at an early age. After a brilliant academic career in psychology and sociology, he became editor of the Johannesburg Nationalist newspaper *Die Transvaler* in 1937, and was appointed a senator (a member of the upper house) in 1948. He became minister of Native affairs in October 1950, his policy being separate development. One of the first actions of his government was the provision of separate universities for non-Whites, the "open" universities, for instance those in Johannesburg and Cape Town, being prohibited from enrolling any more non-White students. As minister of Native affairs Verwoerd had already established, through the Bantu Education Act of 1953, a state-controlled base which gave Black parents a greater say in educational matters and provided syllabuses modified to meet the needs of Black pupils. Previously Black education had been mainly in the

General J. B. M. Hertzog (left), prime minister of the Union from 1924 to 1939, with his trusted supporter since the Second Anglo-Boer War, N. C. Havenga. Havenga was minister of finance from 1924 to 1939 and again from 1948 to 1954.

hands of the Churches and the mission societies.

The keystone to Verwoerd's policy was the Promotion of Self-Government Act of 1959, which divided the many Black territories in South Africa into eight units, and made provision for self-government from which all Whites were to be excluded. This Act also abolished the representation of Blacks in parliament. Henceforth the Blacks were to govern themselves in their own territories.

The National Party's handling of race matters clearly had the support of the White electorate, for the strength of the various Opposition parties declined. While the Labour Party had ceased to exist after 1958, the United Party suffered from a lack of firm leadership after the death of Smuts in 1950. But it did vigorously oppose most apartheid measures. After the election in 1953, three splinter groups of the United Party established themselves without any significant results, and on 13 August 1959 a further split led to the establishment of the Progressive Party, a group of 12 parliamentarians who advocated universal, but qualified suffrage.

Black discontent

There had been signs of Black discontent with White rule long before 1948; the political impotence of the Blacks and their economic disadvantages were fertile ground for Marxism. In existence since the White miners' strike in Johannesburg in 1922, the Communist Party in South Africa not only made attempts to improve the economic and political strength of the non-Whites, but actively fomented strikes, disturbances, anarchy and violence, a situation the Malan government refused to countenance. In 1950 parliament passed the Suppression of Communism Act, which outlawed the party and made the propagation of its ideals a crime. Inevitably, its clandestine operations continued. The same fate lay in store for the African National Congress (ANC), which had been established in 1912 and regarded itself as the only representative of the Black peoples. After 1948 the ANC adopted a provocative policy, calling for what was a partially successful stay-away from work on 1 May 1951. This resulted in clashes between strikers and police when the police attempted to protect non-strikers. Eighteen Blacks lost their lives. Next, the ANC called on the government to revoke six of its discriminatory laws, threatening to protest on 6 April 1952, when South Africa was to celebrate its tercentenary. These demands referred to a "rising tide of bitterness and tension" among the Blacks, and protested against "legislation that continues to insult and degrade the African people".

The government rejected the demands and warned the ANC against the consequences of disrupting law and order. A number of protest meetings were held on 6 April, but a large-scale campaign of civil disobedience began only on 26 June 1952. Over 8 000 Blacks were arrested for ignoring various apartheid measures. Pleading guilty to all charges, they refused to pay fines and elected to serve prison sentences. While the campaign was strictly disciplined, it generated sufficient tension to produce riots which resulted in murder and arson. Thus, at the beginning of 1953, the government enacted two drastic pieces of legislation, one providing for severe penalties in cases of civil disobedience, and the other enabling it to declare a state of emergency in a specific area, or in the country as a whole.

After the watershed election of 1948, South Africa's first three Nationalist prime ministers were (from right to left): Dr D. F. Malan (1948-1954); J. G. Strijdom (1954-1958); and Dr H. F. Verwoerd (1958-1966).

In 1959 a Black section which regarded the ANC as too moderate, broke away to form the Pan-African Congress (PAC), and there were riots throughout the country, the first occurring near Pretoria on 26 February. Early in 1960 the resistance movement became extremely serious and produced the most acute crisis of its kind that South Africa had yet experienced. The PAC encouraged Blacks to go to their nearest police-station and demand arrest for not carrying their identification documents. A large crowd advanced on a police-station at Sharpeville, near Johannesburg, on 21 March and in the rising tension one policeman lost his head. There had been no order to fire, but when his shot rang out it immediately led to a lethal volley, and 69 Blacks were killed. On the same day riots also broke out in Langa, near Cape Town, and elsewhere, and apprehensive Capetonians saw a peaceful procession of 30 000 Blacks move into the centre of their city. The government reacted swiftly by ordering mass arrests, declaring a state of emergency in a large part of the country, and mobilizing part of the Active Citizen Force. It also passed the Unlawful Organizations Act, in effect banning the ANC and PAC. The state of emergency ended on 31 August 1960.

Profoundly shocked, South Africans were stunned a few days later when, on 9 April, Verwoerd was critically wounded in an assassination attempt by a mentally disturbed White. Although twice shot in the head, the premier made a complete recovery.

A BASE FOR A THRIVING ECONOMY

Racial affairs dominate the South African scene to such an extent that equally important matters, such as the country's enormous economic progress, are frequently overlooked. There was an immediate post-war boom, to which the discovery of new goldfields in the northern Orange Free State made a major contribution. Henceforth South Africa's economy was to be based irrevocably on industry rather than on agriculture.

The inflow of foreign capital diminished after the 1948 election, and towards the end of 1949 South Africa, in common with most non-dollar countries, devalued its currency, decreasing the value of the South African £ from $4,03 to $2,80. After this the position gradually improved, but there was a severe setback in 1960, when serious race riots in South Africa and racial friction elsewhere in Africa resulted in the withdrawal of £80 million in private capital from the country.

Yet industrial development from 1948 to 1960 maintained amazing momentum. At the end of this period, 85 per cent of the consumer goods bought in the country was manufactured in South Africa. Apart from the new gold-mines, South Africa also opened its first uranium plant in 1952 and began phosphate-concentrate (fertilizer) production in 1955. This year also saw the beginning of the production of petrol and other petroleum-based products from coal – a particular milestone in South Africa's development because of the energy crisis of the seventies, and the country's almost inexhaustible supply of coal.

The republic referendum

Verwoerd had been concentrating increasingly on attempts to establish unity between the two White groups in South Africa. He believed that this could be achieved only through an independent republic, for which he felt the time was ripe. On 20 January 1960 he announced that a referendum would be held. This was the logical result of the loosening ties with Britain which had developed under his predecessors. In 1949 Malan withdrew South Africans' automatic right to British citizenship, and a year later the right of South Africans to appeal to the British privy council was abolished. Until 1957 the British flag and national anthem had had equal status with South African equivalents, but Strijdom made the latter the sole symbols of South African nationhood. That same year Britain transferred its naval base at Simonstown to the South African government.

The referendum was held on 5 October 1960, and 52 per cent of the voters declared themselves in favour of a republic. Whether he, personally, was convinced that it was necessary or not, Verwoerd firmly intended that South Africa should remain in the Commonwealth, if only to retain the confidence of White, English-speaking South Africans. For membership he required the approval of the Commonwealth prime ministers' conference, which was held in March 1961 at Lancaster House, London. Severe criticism of South Africa's race policy by some Commonwealth premiers threatened to cause a schism in this loosely associated body, and, so as not to be an embarrassment to the older and more conservative members, Verwoerd had no choice but to withdraw his country's application for continued membership.

The triumph of republicanism: Charles Robberts Swart addresses the crowd on Church Square, Pretoria, on 31 May 1961 after being sworn in as first state president of the Republic of South Africa. On the left is a reminder of a bygone republican era: the statue of Paul Kruger, last president of the Zuid-Afrikaansche Republiek.

A republic for the eighties

When the Republic of South Africa was formally proclaimed on 31 May 1961, with the former governor-general, C. R. Swart, sworn in as state president to uphold what had been the constitution of the Union of South Africa, it represented the final triumph of republicanism and of Afrikaner nationalism. Republicanism had held firm in the difficult years following the Anglo-Boer War (1899-1902), despite and probably because of Lord Milner's determined efforts to impose British supremacy on the country. It had been accepted as a party principle by Dr D. F. Malan's National Party before the Second World War (this being a major difference with General Hertzog), and before his retirement as prime minister in 1954 Malan had loosened ties with Britain further. After 1949 South Africans were no longer British citizens automatically, and a year later the right of appeal to the British privy council was abolished. Malan's successor, J. G. Strijdom, loosened these ties still more, and although there was some surprise when Dr. H. F. Verwoerd, who became prime minister in 1958, announced the republic referendum, he

had gauged the public mood correctly. A comfortable majority in favour of a republic was obtained.

There had been a growing consolidation of the South Africanism of the two White language groups, largely due to external threats. The Soviet Union and Communist China had increased their activity elsewhere in Africa, and at the United Nations and other international forums South Africa was coming under increasing attack. The Third World and the Communist countries contested South Africa's League of Nations mandate in South-West Africa, and international isolation of South Africa in fields such as sport, culture and co-operation was growing. Verwoerd believed that these challenges could be faced only if the White electorate followed a common ideal.

Black nationalism

But Black nationalism was also growing into a force to be reckoned with. The shots which had

The South African Defence Force is generally regarded as the continent's most formidable military force and, partly because of the mandatory U.N. arms embargo against the Republic, she produces most of her weaponry internally. These Impala jets were manufactured by the Atlas aircraft factory.

NATIONAL PARTY SUPREMACY SINCE 1948

Until the election of 1943 the National Party had had an absolute majority only once: this was in 1929 under the leadership of General Hertzog. The watershed was 1948, under the leadership of Dr Malan, when the party, already dedicated to republicanism, gained an outright majority with the support of Havenga's Afrikaner Party, with which it merged in 1951.

From 1948 the Opposition was essentially the United Party, which finally crumbled away in 1977, weakened by internal dissension and abandoned by most English-language newspapers. An earlier splintering in the late fifties engendered the Progressive Party, and in 1977 the New Republic Party as well as the South African Party were founded. The latter soon merged with the National Party.

The National Party is, however, not without its internal dissensions. This can be seen in the campaigns for a foothold in Parliament, unsuccessful until now, of the *Herstigte* ("reconstituted") National Party (established in 1969) and, since 1980, in the emergence of another right-wing group, the National Conservative Party.

The following table indicates the seats gained by parties at each general election since 1948. Explanations applicable to the table for the elections up to 1948 (p. 50) also apply here.

	1948	1953	1958	1961	1966	1970	1974	1977	1981
National	70	94	103	105	126	118	123	134	131
United	65	57	53	49	39	47	41		
Labour	6	4							
Afrikaner	9								
Progressive				1	1	1	7	17	26
National Union			1						
SAP								3	
NRP								10	8

The State President and his wife in front of the main entrance to the Houses of Parliament in Cape Town after the opening of a new parliamentary session. With Union in 1910 Cape Town became the legislative capital of South Africa. Its parliament buildings, although the biggest in the country, were too small for the new legislative body and had to be extended. The original building was completed in 1879 and officially opened by Sir Hercules Robinson, then governor of the Cape Colony. Since 1910 further extensions to the building became necessary on various occasions.

echoed round the world from Sharpeville in 1960 caused the government to declare a state of emergency and to ban the PAC and the ANC as unlawful organizations. But these measures also resulted in growing support from Black nationalism elsewhere in Africa, as well as continued Communist subversion. In a speech to the South African parliament on 3 February 1960, Britain's prime minister, Harold Macmillan, had already referred prophetically to "winds of change" blowing through Africa, but while he was referring to legitimate Black aspirations, it was clear to South African security experts that it was Communism which largely was generating those winds.

The Communist Party had been outlawed in South Africa under the Suppression of Communism Act of 1950, and had gone underground, working hand in glove with the PAC and ANC. Exploitation of Black nationalism resulted in subversive activities against the government which included the incitement of labour unrest and the creation of a militant wing of the PAC called Poqo. The Communist command post within South Africa was unearthed on a farm at Rivonia, near Johannesburg, this leading in 1964 and 1965 to the arrest and trial of leaders who included a number of Whites, and a crackdown on leftist student participation. Outbreaks of subversion, supported by terrorist activity, recur sporadically at the instigation of cells outside South Africa, although there is little evidence of organized militarized movements such as the short-lived *Umkhonto we Sizwe* (Spear of the Nation).

The first visible signs of an assertive expression of Black consciousness involving the exclusion of Whites – even those supporting Black nationalism – came with the establishment of the South African Students' Organization in 1969.

The Soweto riots

The most recent large-scale manifestation of Black consciousness, the result of organized agitation and intimidation according to the subsequent judicial commission of inquiry, came in June 1976. In urban Black areas pupils boycotted and in many cases burned down their schools, the unrest lasting nine months. The commission found that the immediate cause was official insistence that Afrikaans should be on an equal footing with English as a medium of instruction in Black schools, and blamed education officials for ignoring the danger signals. The police, the commission said, should have anticipated violence and taken counter-measures. Contributory factors behind the unrest were issues such as discrimination, citizen-

The towering lights of the Sasol II plant. Sasol became the world's first economically viable oil-from-coal enterprise when it started producing petrol from coal in 1955 in the Orange Free State. When oil prices rocketed in the seventies it was decided to build a second Sasol in the Eastern Transvaal on a large coalfield near Trichardt. Together these two plants will produce a substantial portion of the Republic's liquid fuel needs.

ship, restrictions on land ownership, and lack of facilities, declared the commission.

There were isolated outbreaks of violence and rising tension when the Soweto riots, as they became known, were commemorated a year later. On 12 September 1977 Steve Biko, president of the Black People's Convention and a leading voice of the agitators, died in detention. At the public inquest it was found that nobody could be held legally responsible for his death.

Opposition politics

While the policy of the government has been clearly endorsed by most of the White voters, that of the Progressive Party, which became the Progressive Federal Party (PFP) in 1977, seemed for a long time to be a lost cause. Represented in parliament by a single member, Mrs Helen Suzman, from 1961 to 1974, when its representation increased to seven, the party based its proposals for an integrated government chiefly on a qualified franchise. With the demise of the United Party in 1977, the PFP won 17 seats. In this election the National Party secured its largest majority ever (134 seats) while another opposition group, the New Republic Party (NRP), emerged with ten seats. The NRP prefers maximum local autonomy for each community in a consociational or confederal structure.

The PFP has become a strong advocate for a national convention (consisting of the leaders of all South African peoples) which would draft a constitution guaranteeing non-negotiable minority rights. In the general elections of April 1981 the PFP achieved the most material gains with 26 seats. The Nationalists were slightly reduced to 131, and the NRP to eight. However, a now significant body of right-wing opinion, basically dedicated to the ideals of old-style apartheid, emerged in 1981 without gaining parliamentary representation.

Forces militating against polarization are at

work, however. On the one hand there is the considerable body of moderate opinion among the Blacks which rejects revolution as a means to obtain more political rights and has opted for dialogue. This, on the other hand, is matched by a greater realization by some Whites that there should be adaptation of traditional policy within the limits imposed by preservation of identity and the protection of minority rights.

Contacts with Black Africa

A bold measure which Verwoerd cautiously inaugurated and his successor, B. J. Vorster, pursued with vigour, was a search for understanding among Black African states. To this end Verwoerd conferred with the prime minister of Lesotho, Chief Leabua Jonathan, in September 1966. In September 1968, two years after Vorster had succeeded Verwoerd, Malawi became the first Black African state to establish normal diplomatic relations with South Africa. This was followed by Vorsters's visit to Malawi in May 1970 and a reciprocal visit by Malawi's head of state, Dr Kamuzu Banda, to South Africa in 1971.

Towards the end of 1974 Vorster devoted a vital speech in the senate, the upper house of the South African parliament, to a firm policy of détente with Black Africa, mentioning one of its most vigorous critics, Zambia, under President Kenneth Kaunda. Vorster paid a visit, initially secret, to President Felix Houphouët-Boigny of the Ivory Coast in

September 1974, and in February 1975 discussions were held with the then president of Liberia, William Tolbert. In pursuit of a settlement of the crisis in neighbouring Rhodesia, a dramatic meeting was held between Kaunda and Vorster in a railway-carriage stationed on the Victoria Falls bridge.

Despite their political differences there are substantial links between South Africa and other African countries. These include infrastructural services and transportation, labour, trade and agriculture, as well as development co-operation and investments. South Africa's exports to the rest of the African continent in 1980 were valued at R1 100 million, 50 per cent more than those of the year before, food being one of the most important elements.

As the continent's most highly industrialized state South Africa not only has capital and consumer goods for export, but an almost unlimited range of technical and scientific expertise which it repeatedly offers to share with all Black African states. South Africa has rail links with several contiguous countries under Black rule: Mozambique, Zimbabwe (formerly Rhodesia), Botswana, Lesotho, Swaziland, and, through Zimbabwe, with Zambia and Zaire. Hydro-electric projects are shared with Angola and Mozambique, and another has been planned in co-operation with Lesotho.

Luxury rail travel: The world-famous Blue Train, pride of the South African Railways, on its 1 600 km journey between Pretoria and Cape Town. South Africa's railway system is pre-eminent in Africa. It accounts for 24 000 km (25 percent) of Africa's 93 000 km railroads. The South African Railways carry about two-thirds of all freight hauled by rail in Africa, much of it originating in or destined for countries as far north as Zaire. All rolling stock, with the exception of some locomotives, are manufactured locally.

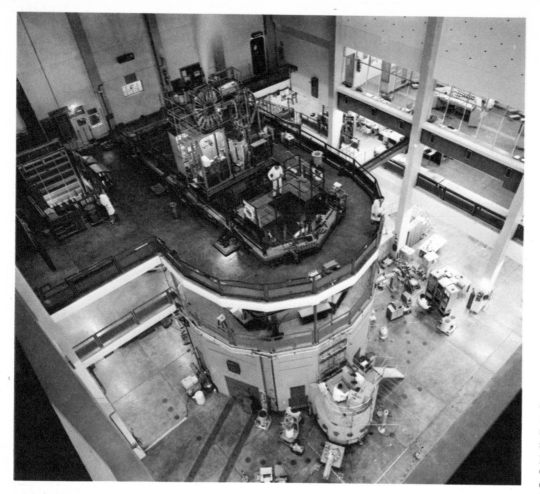

The hall of the Safari I nuclear reactor at Pelindaba, near Pretoria, which 16 years ago ushered South Africa into the nuclear age. The Republic is one of the three largest producers of uranium in the world and its reserves of uranium metal are ranked fourth in the West. The country's scientists have developed a new process for the enrichment of uranium for use in nuclear reactors and conduct important research on the peaceful application of nuclear technology. South Africa's first nuclear power-station, built near Cape Town, is due to come into operation in the early 1980s.

African prime minister then visited. His successor, P. W. Botha, continued this policy by extending formal relations with the Republic of China (Taiwan); this also resulted in a personal visit in 1981.

Steady, impressive industrial growth

The continuing industrialization of South Africa took place chiefly because of the stimulus provided by needs resulting from the Second World War. It is the economic basis for external relationships and an important internal determinant. The fifties saw steady and impressive industrial growth, briefly halted by a mass flight of capital after the events of Sharpeville in 1960 and after the establishment of a republic the following year. Defended by exchange and import controls, the economy recovered to maintain, during the sixties, a growth rate that surpassed that of most other countries. In the early seventies expansion was hampered after a short period of excessive speculation on the stock exchange and, by the middle of the decade, as in all developed countries, by the sudden rise in prices for fossil fuels. South Africa, however, possesses large reserves of coal and has the world's largest commercially viable fuel-from-coal industry, which is rapidly expanding. A systematic search for oil began in 1964.

Industrialization leads inevitably to urbanization. Between Union (1910) and Republic (1961) no less than 84 per cent of the White population became urbanized. (More than 53 per cent of Whites were urbanized in 1904.) This relates

An outright enemy: international Communism

Living at best in uneasy alliance with most of the West and, chiefly through trade links, with some Black African states, South Africa still has to contend with an outright enemy: international Communism from the Soviet Union and China. If South Africa's strategic position on a vital sea route is important to Communist plans for world domination, her many strategic minerals are as attractive. In this context South-West Africa/Namibia has become an increasingly sensitive area, since the Soviet Union actively supports the South-West African People's Organization (SWAPO), which hopes to seize power in the territory.

Self-determination for the inhabitants of South-West Africa/Namibia has been dragged through international forums for years. Meanwhile, under South African guidance, a self-governing body has been established in the territory after thorough constitutional consultations between all the indigenous groups and a free one man, one vote election in December 1978. International discussions about the status of the territory have been severely hampered by the possibility of United Nations partiality in favour of SWAPO in a proposed election under international supervision.

Angola is the other area in which an overt Communist presence is a threat to peace in southern

Africa. On behalf of the Soviet Union Cuba is maintaining some 30 000 troops in Angola, and there are many East German "technical advisers" in both Angola and Mozambique.

Under these circumstances South Africa seeks new friends and allies with deliberate caution. Under Vorster ties were established in South America with Chile and Paraguay and, most notably, in April 1976 with Israel, which the South

Prime Minister P. W. Botha, second from left, with his minister of co-operation and development, Dr Piet Koornhof, during talks with the chief ministers of the Black national states of Gazankulu and Lebowa, Professor Hudson Ntsanwisi, second from right, and Dr Cedric Phatudi respectively. Gazankulu is the national state of the Machangana-Tsonga and Lebowa that of the North Sotho.

principally to the Afrikaners, who have in consequence considerably increased their stake in the economy. In numbers, White urbanization was far exceeded by that of the Blacks. In 1936 about 51 per cent of the total population was engaged in agriculture. By 1970 the figure had dropped to 13 per cent. Urbanization has been accompanied by marked improvements in living standards which, *per capita* for the whole population, are far higher than those for Black Africa.

The evolution of apartheid

During the National Party's uninterrupted tenure of government from 1948, when the word "apartheid" (separateness) gained international currency, attempts to satisfy Black aspirations have increased considerably. The preceding Smuts government had adopted what essentially was a *laissez-faire* attitude towards race relations, although it is certain that General Smuts knew that this was the country's most important internal problem. The first measures of Dr Malan's new government after the 1948 elections were a series of laws ensuring social segregation between White and non-White. There were to be separate facilities; inter-racial marriages were made illegal; and territorial separation in residential areas was to be enforced. Behind this policy was the view that segregation was essential if White civilization was to be maintained in South Africa, and if the Whites were to retain their right to determine their own fate.

The undoubted architect of a more positive and creative response to the problem of separating the races was Dr H. F. Verwoerd, first as minister of Native affairs (1950-1958) and then as prime minister (1958-1966). Verwoerd stressed that his government would provide fair and just opportunities for Black development and this policy became known as separate development. Inherent in this view is the recognition that the Blacks of southern Africa are not and have never been a homogeneous nation, but represent several distinct ethnic identities which, together with the Whites, form a plural society which also includes Coloured people and Asians. Nor have White or Black had any prior historical claim to the whole of South Africa's territory.

In January 1962 Verwoerd's Black homeland policy started to take shape. What had hitherto been known as Native reserves became, in accordance with traditional occupation, the recognized homelands of their inhabitants who were to be given a measure of self-government leading to eventual political independence. The first self-gov-

Mining headgear. South Africa is a treasure-house of those minerals that are the very life-blood of the industrialized societies of the West. It has 75% of the world's known platinum, chrome and vanadium reserves, 50% of all gold and 78% of all manganese reserves, 18% of the Western world's uranium reserves, 20% of all industrial diamonds and about 8% of all nickel, zinc and phosphates. South Africa is also a major coal exporter.

Most of South Africa's coal is used to generate electricity, and most electricity used in South Africa is supplied by the Electricity Supply Commission (ESCOM). It has established a national high-voltage grid to supply power to virtually every corner of the country, as well as to several neighbouring countries. ESCOM has about twenty large coal-fired power-stations with several new stations being planned.

59

A FREE SEA TRADE-ROUTE FOR THE WEST

South Africa's quest for an orderly and peaceful existence is confined not only to the resolution of internal issues, but to pressing international problems. Geographically poised at the end of the African continent, in a position midway between East and West, South Africa has for centuries been strategically the most important safeguard of a free sea trade-route. Yet while Western nations energetically support the principle of a safe sea route round the Cape, on which they depend to a large extent, they have come under increasing Black attack in international forums for their overt or tacit co-operation with a country whose internal policies do not gain international acceptance, either in the highly industrialized West or in predominantly agricultural Black Africa, although for both world trade is of prime importance.

Durban is South Africa's busiest port and forms an important link in the southern sea route which is the Western world's oil lifeline. The passenger mailship in the picture is a romantic legacy of past years.

erning legislative assembly was introduced in Transkei in 1963, but Verwoerd was not destined to see the total fulfilment of his ideas.

On 6 September 1966 South Africa was stunned by the assassination of the man who in the previous 17 years had, probably more than any other, put his personal stamp on the country's internal policies. On the eve of what, it was expected, would have been a major policy announcement, Verwoerd was stabbed to death in his seat in parliament by a temporary messenger of foreign extraction who was subsequently found to be mentally unfit to stand trial.

Transkei becomes independent

The Black homeland policy had been firmly established during Verwoerd's term of office, but it developed still further under Vorster. Transkei became an independent state on 26 October 1976. Bophuthatswana followed (6 December 1977), as did Venda (13 September 1979), and Ciskei (4 December 1981). There are six other self-governing Black territories in South Africa: KwaZulu, Kwa-Ndebele, KaNgwane, Qwaqwa, Gazankulu and Lebowa. Economically Whites and Blacks in South Africa are interdependent, the effect of this being large Black populations in White urban industrial areas. In 1977 these Blacks were given local autonomy through the establishment of community councils. By August 1978 altogether 103 of these councils had been established, with about 280 envisaged. In 1979 Blacks in White urban areas were given the right to acquire 99-year leaseholds on residential and business properties.

These steps can be seen as the positive acknowledgement by the government of the permanence of Black populations in urban industrialized areas, a situation that calls for far-reaching social adjustments. While the government is committed to

The Hartebeesthoek earth-satellite tracking station near Pretoria. South Africa's telecommunications system is the most modern in Africa. Hartebeesthoek was opened in 1975 and links the country to the Atlantic Ocean satellite system. Later a second antenna link-up with the Indian Ocean system and a third antenna to augment the Atlantic system were installed. Thus instant communication of high quality is available to virtually all parts of the world.

In practice housing in South Africa is provided jointly by the state and private enterprise, the latter usually meeting the needs of those in the higher income groups who can afford to finance their own homes. Above left is Mitchells Plain near Cape Town, that will eventually accommodate 250 000 Coloured people in about 40 000 dwellings. On the right is a Black housing scheme at East London.

developing the Black states to which it has given self-rule, and which it is consolidating, it is government policy that proprietors in White areas should decide for themselves whether amenities such as hotels and restaurants should be available to all races. Many theatres have been declared open to all races. This holds good for sport: all national events are multiracial, this resulting recently in the selection of the first non-White Springbok rugby-player.

Meanwhile the social conditions of non-Whites have improved considerably. The number of Black pupils in primary and secondary schools has risen from 1 500 000 to almost 3 500 000 during the past two decades. What is of much greater significance is the fact that pupils in matriculation classes have increased from 700 in 1960 to 43 000 in 1980. It is equally important that from 1950 to 1979 pupils in secondary schools have increased fivefold – from 101 000 to 508 000.

From 1965 to 1980 the number of Coloured school pupils doubled, rising from 380 000 to 750 000. During these 15 years pupils in secondary schools trebled, increasing from 64 000 to 188 000. Asian pupils in all primary and secondary schools have increased from 155 000 to 218 000 between 1965 and 1980. At the same time, moreover, matriculation classes have grown by nearly 300 per cent, rising from 2 000 pupils to 7 500.

The government assumes responsibility for all Whites, Coloureds, Asians and Blacks outside the national states who cannot buy or build their own houses. Only income and circumstances, not race or colour, determine whether or not a person qualifies for state aid in housing. In the first five years since its inception in 1975, the National Housing Fund has provided R1 816 million for the construction of 653 931 housing units, an average of nearly 130 000 houses a year. Of these, 60 580 (9,3 per cent of the total) have been built for Indians, 73 605 (11,3 per cent) for Whites, 213 119 (32,6 per cent) for Coloureds, and 306 627 (46,8 per cent) for Blacks.

A specialist medical team from South Africa on a weekend visit to the neighbouring Black state of Lesotho. This weekend shuttle service has been in operation since the late 1960s. Specialists and nurses offer their services free of charge and transport is provided by a major South African industrial group.

A MAGNA CARTA FOR HEALTH

South Africa's new Magna Carta for health services came into operation in 1977. Today there is equal emphasis on promotive, preventive, curative and rehabilitation services for all population groups in a new, integrated approach.

Prevention and treatment of communicable diseases such as tuberculosis, leprosy, typhoid, malaria and venereal diseases are the responsibility of the state. Treatment is free. Free psychiatric services are also provided by the state, the exception being voluntary patients, who pay a nominal fee. Public health services provided by provincial councils or local authorities are either free, or each patient pays according to his means. Most Blacks pay only a nominal fee of 50 cents for medical services.

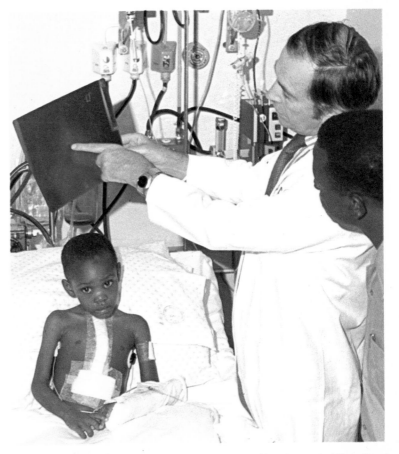

Professor Chris Barnard and a Kenyan child who received heart surgery at Cape Town's famous Groote Schuur Hospital. Since Professor Barnard performed the world's first heart-transplant operation at Groote Schuur in the late 1960s this hospital has been world-famous, especially for its heart surgery. South Africa's leadership in medicine in Africa is regularly acknowledged whenever a problem situation arises which requires scientific medical expertise of a very high order. Patients from neighbouring Black states and further afield are often treated in South African hospitals.

The University of South Africa (UNISA), the largest correspondence university in the world. It is situated in Pretoria and has thousands of foreign students, many of them from other states in Southern Africa.

The Southern Africa Medical University (MEDUNSA) at Ga-Rankuwa near Pretoria, which trains Black doctors, dentists, veterinarians and other medical personnel. It accepts students from all over Southern Africa.

The Coloured and Asian communities

The rights and interests of the Coloured and Asian communities are proving more of a problem than those for Blacks, primarily because neither group has a distinct geographic homeland as a base. Both form part of the multi-ethnic urban communities of most major cities. Coloured people were represented in parliament on a common voters' roll until 1956, when the roll was abolished by the government after a lengthy constitutional struggle. On a separate roll Coloureds were given the opportunity of electing four Whites who specifically represented their interests. But in 1964 the government announced its intention of establishing a totally separate Coloured Persons' Representative Council (CRC), the first elections being held on 24 September 1969. The council did not prove to be a viable solution. Stalemate between the government and the CRC resulted, with anti-government opinion in the council demanding participation in the central government.

In one of the most comprehensive and penetrating studies of community relations in South Africa's history, the Theron Commission on Coloured Affairs reported to parliament at the end of 1976 that there would have to be more meaningful participation in the political system. Separate parliaments for White, Coloured and Indian (Asian) people – suggested by a cabinet sub-committee in 1977 – were rejected by the CRC and the South African Indian Council (SAIC). Meanwhile the CRC remains suspended at its own request, but individual members of the Coloured community serve on numerous consultative government bodies.

In 1961 the government acknowledged that the Indians had to be considered a permanent part of the population. The South African Indian Council was formed in 1964: at first a nominated, but since 1972 a partly elected body with advisory powers. The first elections were held in November 1974. But on the whole the council has followed the course of the CRC and has been suspended while the government's proposals for constitutional reform take shape.

Consultative forums for the future

South Africa's present prime minister, P. W. Botha, took office on 28 September 1978 amidst the so-called Information Scandal, in which the misappropriation of public funds was investigated and proved by a judicial commission whose report was considered by an extraordinary session of parliament. After the death of Dr N. Diederichs, who held the office of state president from 1975, Vorster was elected state president, but shortly afterwards retired from public life, to be succeeded by Marais Viljoen on 29 June 1979.

In the main, Prime Minister Botha's resolute leadership has given formal shape to the pressing need for consultative forums regarding South Africa's future. The first step towards the creation of such forums was the abolition of the upper house of parliament, the senate, and the introduction of a nominated president's council which has Coloured and Asian members. The chairman is the vice-president, a new office held by A. L. Schlebusch. The government has excluded Blacks from participation in the council on the grounds that they are already consulted through their own self-governing bodies. This decision does not enjoy the support of the Progressive Federal Party (PFP), which advocates a national convention that is fully representative. The council, which is divided into five committees (constitutional, economic, scientific, planning and community relations), has the wide-ranging task of advising the state president on any matter which, in its opinion, is of public importance. Devising plans for a new political future for Coloureds and Asians for submission to the government is clearly the council's major task.

Salient features of a twelve-point plan formulated by Prime Minister Botha in August 1979 are acceptance of the principle of "vertical differentiation", together with self-determination, in as many areas as possible; the removal of hurtful discrimination; and the creation of a constellation of states of southern Africa with respect for one

State President Marais Viljoen and Vice-President A. L. Schlebusch at the opening of the president's council, a nominated consultative body comprising White, Coloured and Asian members that was created after the upper house of parliament, the senate, was abolished. The council can advise the state president on any matter of public importance.

Tourism is a major industry in South Africa and one of the most popular areas is the Natal north coast, on the warm Indian Ocean.

South Africa and South-West Africa/Namibia are the only food-exporting countries on the African continent. Wheat is one of the staple foods exported to many African countries.

another's point of view. In this way justice and economic progress would ensure the stability which was the best defence against Marxist incursions. In November 1979 Botha enlisted the aid of private enterprise for his plans by convening a meeting of about 250 leading businessmen.

This meeting, known as the Carlton Conference, was Botha's platform for outlining in detail his concept of a constellation of states. He said that the constellation could include any country in the African subcontinent that acknowledged the need to expand relationships and co-operate on a regional basis. That did not imply a formal organization, but a grouping of states with mutual interests and growing inter-relationships.

Replying to a no-confidence debate in parliament later, the prime minister said that the con-stellation might take the form of a confederation linked by a council of states. Preparations for an inter-state secretariat which would pave the way for such a council had begun. All independent national Black states would qualify for full membership of the council on a basis of equality. Self-governing territories which had not yet become independent or had refused independence could be granted associate membership and given observer status at the deliberations of the council while they would still be represented by South Africa.

Turning to urban Blacks, the prime minister said that he hoped it would be possible for most of them to be represented in the Council of States by the delegates from the national states from which they had originated. "But if there are others who for practical reasons cannot be accommodated in this way, they may be given a say in the deliberations of the council of states in some co-ordinated manner or other," the prime minister said.

Role of economics

Outlining the part he felt private enterprise could play, Botha stressed at the Carlton Conference the need for a more equitable distribution of economic activity which would include the self-governing Black territories, but rejected the "development aid" supplied elsewhere in Africa. He believed firmly in the long-term advantages to be derived from the creation of new opportunities for work, advantages which meant not only financial but also political and socio-economic stability.

Economics could well prove to be one of the major determinants of the political future of southern Africa, for industrial progress without better labour resources is impossible. In a far-reaching and fundamental manner, often seemingly unnoticed, labour legislation is altering the traditional fabric of South African society. Recognizing the urgent need for the improvement of skills and opportunities, the government appointed the Wiehahn Commission to report on labour legislation and future needs. It was the first multiracial body on which all four of the official population groups were represented. With the Industrial Conciliation Amendment Act of 19 June 1979 some of the commission's sweeping recommendations have been implemented, while others have been accepted in principle.

Workers now have full freedom of association; existing Black unions can register for recognition; registered unions are admitted to industrial councils; job reservation (by which certain trades were reserved for Whites) has largely been phased out; and workers and their employers can now determine for themselves their facilities in shops and offices, whereas previously segregated facilities were mandatory.

A National Manpower Commission has been appointed, and among other matters it will discuss the implementation of the accepted principles of making available apprenticeships to all races in all areas, and the encouragement of training in industrial relations. The extent to which such provisions, above all, succeed in satisfying the aspirations for an improved quality of life for all the communities in South Africa could decide the future peace and prosperity of the country.

South Africa has almost 1,5 million industrial employees of whom three-quarters are not White. There are over 15 000 factories in the country. In the early 1980s South Africa's labour laws were substantially overhauled and amended. These changes were mainly inspired by two important commissions of enquiry whose reports were accepted by the Government.

Index